THE 10-MINUTE
MILLIONAIRE

THE 10-MINUTE
MILLIONAIRE

THE ONE SECRET
ANYONE CAN USE
TO TURN $2,500 INTO
$1 MILLION OR MORE

D. R. BARTON, JR.

WILEY

ISBN 978-1-118-85670-3 (Hardcover)
ISBN 978-1-118-85691-8 (ePDF)
ISBN 978-1-118-85680-2 (ePub)

Printed in the United States of America.

10 9 8 7 6 5 4 3 2 1

My life is in the hands of my Lord, Jesus Christ. My heart and my eternal thanks belong to my amazing wife, Cathie. My admiration goes out to Meg and Josh, who continue to deserve it every day. My gratitude belongs to my dad, who has inspired me, believed in me, and shown me how to live.

Along with everything that I do, this book is dedicated to you.

CONTENTS

FOREWORD

I n a recent survey by BlackRock, Inc., the world's largest money-management firm, 74 percent of respondents said that they expect to feel financially secure in their retirement. However, there's a $30,000-a-year income gap between what they need and what their savings will earn.

During our educational webinars, when we ask participants what their biggest concerns are, we consistently hear that market volatility creates intense anxiety for traders and investors alike.

When you combine these responses, what you get is a large group of Americans who need to be successful in the stock market to grow their nest egg and fund their retirement, especially in the current environment of historically low interest rates. However, because of concerns over market volatility and a distrust of Wall Street, the average investor has sat out the seven-year bull market that began in 2009. Some pundits have called this the most-unloved bull market in history.

What investors and traders need is a disciplined methodology that gives them the confidence and conviction to be in the stock market, not on the sidelines. D. R. Barton, Jr. has researched and developed just such a plan.

I have known D.R. for more than 20 years. In that time, I have come to respect not just his trading acumen but also his integrity ... in life and in his trading system research. What he has done in *The 10-Minute Millionaire* is to bring together three disciplines that are essential to success in the stock market:

1. A high-probability trading plan with well-defined entries and exits.
2. A focus on money management and risk management.
3. A plan that allows traders to take advantage of volatility—and not be spooked by it.

What D.R. has put together is a trading plan that positions you for success. He understands that focus is the key to success in the stock market. Focus leads to conviction and conviction empowers you with the confidence you need to follow the trading plan religiously, like all successful traders do.

I have compared the quest for a consistently reliable trading system to the search for intelligent life in our universe ... we know it's probably out there but it's darn hard to find. D.R. has taken one big step in the right direction with *The 10-Minute Millionaire*.

—Marc Chaikin
Founder and CEO, Chaikin Analytics LLC
August 2016

[Editor's Note: Marc Chaikin is a legend in the super-competitive world of technical market analysis. His groundbreaking work includes the development of the Chaikin Money Flow and Chaikin Oscillator indicators—both industry standards found in virtually all the widely used charting-software platforms. Chaikin is now building an even greater legacy through his new venture at Chaikin Analytics LLC. His latest quantitative, fundamental and technical-analysis models are being used in market-beating indexes at the Nasdaq, on institutional trading desks, and by individual investors throughout the world.]

ACKNOWLEDGMENTS

The first money I ever earned was the $5 I got for mowing Mr. Campbell's yard back when I was 10.

Mr. Campbell was a neighbor of ours, and I remember that he had one of the all-time great nicknames: Soup. (I just called him "Mr. Campbell.")

That nickname isn't all that I remember from those childhood days in Virginia. I also remember all the people who helped me get those jobs done . . . as well as the lawn-mowing dollars that followed.

Back then, my dad let me borrow the push lawn mower. Mom would run me down to the Esso station for gas anytime I ran low. And when I was away on vacation, I knew I could count on friends—like close buddy Rob, or Mike, the little brother of another friend—to cover my commitments.

Because I had a great team, by the time I was a senior in high school, I was mowing 14 lawns per week—even when holding down a full-time summer job in the city of Radford electrical department.

Lawns were meticulously mowed (people just love straight lines—that's how I got all those terrific referrals). I made good money for college. And I always thanked everyone who helped me. I was especially grateful to my dad, who provided mowers and maintenance and eventually the use of our 1968 Ford Torino Squire station wagon so I could expand my territory. And my back-ups were always there when I needed them.

I learned a valuable lesson here ... and I learned it early. Ever since that very first job, I've been getting projects done by working with talented and caring teams.

The projects have run the gamut: at work, at church, volunteering at schools, even starting and coaching sports teams. And in every one of those endeavors, the whole was greater than the sum of the parts.

The 10-Minute Millionaire is another of my team success stories. There are people who I've worked with for decades in the trading and investing world and I stand on their shoulders. That background has combined with the talented people who helped to make this book project a reality to produce an end result that is—once again—greater than the sum of its parts. And because of that, it's certainly much more useful and enjoyable than anything I could have done on my own.

Mike Ward is brilliant. He is the founder and publisher of Money Map Press, and is an amazing idea man and gifted marketer. When it comes to understanding the complex synthesis of people, publishing, and financial markets—Mike is without peer. This book project is his brainchild, right down to the title. Mike, thanks for your support, your guidance, and your leadership. And most of all, thanks for being such a great friend for more than decade.

Bill Patalon is a selfless genius. His vision is what makes this book what it is today.

When it comes to communicating any topic, Bill can find both the key concept and the hidden nuggets of gold scattered about and turn them into a glorious unified whole that trips lightly off the tongue. I had a bunch of ideas. Bill culled them and massaged them and created a continuity of message that will both resonate and be useful for many a reader. I have never had the honor to work so closely with a man who has such tenacity and talent. I've made friends in numerous ways before, but jumping directly into the trenches with Bill has been one of the most satisfying befriending experiences I've ever had. Bill, from the bottom of my heart, thanks for the many long nights, the even more numerous brilliant insights, and for pouring a large chunk of yourself into this book. I'll continue to treasure our weekly market-review phone calls for as long as you're willing to have them.

I met Andrew Greta two full years ago. We hit it off immediately. Andrew has an amazing combination of abilities—he can conceptualize ideas at a high level and dig into the nitty-gritty details. A rare medley of skills. Andrew had the unenviable task of pulling more information out of me than I knew was in there. His creative, editorial, and analytical inputs were indispensable during this project. Andrew, thanks for all your contributions, both large and small (and there were lots of both). I deeply appreciated your calm and accepting demeanor no matter what chaos was going on around you. And I look forward to collaborating on many projects with you in the future.

Every project has unsung heroes. Terry Weiss has shown his leadership in so many ways through this process. A key player in the structuring (and re-structuring) of the book, his guidance has been felt in many ways. Terry, I really appreciate your nonstop encouragement, your positive leadership, and your foresight for all of the possibilities from here.

Stephanie Bills probably didn't expect to see her name here. But without her steady and skilled hand at the helm of my trading newsletter, I could not have given as much attention to this book. Steph—it's been a joy watching you develop your skills and talents. Thanks for having my back. And I'm looking forward to bringing all the new projects we have on our plate to fruition.

Truly insightful concepts are hard to find. So when I needed a really big unifying story for this book, I went to the most exceptional mind that I know. Meg Barton is my daughter, but I thank the Good Lord that she got her smarts and her looks from her mom. She has more ability in her pinky than most people have in their whole bodies. Early in the writing process, I was stuck trying to find an example that would tie the book together, a concept that would readily describe the importance of preparation in being able to do things efficiently. I gave the problem to Meg. She is the researcher who found the story of Huck's Defeat and so elegantly tied it into the importance that 10 minutes can play in our lives. Meg—you make me proud. Thanks for pulling together the key story for the book. You're amazing and I love you. I can't wait to see what you do next.

My son, Josh, was helping with this book before he even knew it. In high school and college he taught himself how to code. So when I needed some programming work, I asked if he'd like to learn a new programming language. He quickly agreed. So Josh is the guy who turned all of the trading rules into lines of code for much of the really deep research that I did long before I started using the 10-Minute Millionaire strategy in real time. Josh is not doing much programming now: he's in the first year of his MD/PhD track at medical school. Josh—I love you and you make me proud. Thanks for your meticulous programming and research work that helped refine and simplify the 10-Minute Millionaire strategy.

I know you're ready to change the world and I can't wait to watch you do it.

There are lots of people who can do detailed technical work at a very high level. And there are those who can think strategically and really understand the big picture. But there are precious few who can do both. Fortunately, I married one of the precious few. Cathie Barton has been my best friend, my spiritual lighthouse, and the most fun person to be around since the day we met (the day before college classes started our freshman year). She is the mom to two amazing children (see the preceding). She's also a PhD civil/environmental engineer and a global leader in issues management. But all of that is easy compared to putting up with me, especially during a project. Yet Cathie has always been the voice of reason and the consultant I most trust to ask about any of the tough questions during the book writing process. Cathie, thanks for sharing insights, problem solving, and helping me stay focused on the right thing. In you, God has blessed me beyond my wildest dreams.

My dad is featured in several stories throughout this book. That's because he has always been and continues to be the man I most admire. I need look no further for a model of integrity, of how to be a good dad to your children and of how to have fun, enjoy life, and still keep yourself centered. My dad has provided me with encouragement and inspiration throughout this process. Dad, thanks for showing me the way instead of just telling me the way. If everyone had a dad like you, this world would be a much better place.

My brother, Douglas Barton, has always been there for me throughout the project to help research and conceptualize ideas. Douglas has a great knowledge of the financial markets, which he shares with his banking clients, my dad, and me. Many of the things that he worked on have been saved for later publication, but I am grateful for his contributions and willingness to help.

There is a whole host of people who have taught me invaluable lessons about the financial markets.

I met Dr. Van K. Tharp at one of his seminars two decades ago. He taught me so much about the psychology of trading, risk management, and many other topics directly and indirectly related to the markets. We started a seminar company together, wrote a book together, and taught together. Van and I have kept and grown our friendship through trying times and triumphant times and his work continues to inspire me.

Christopher Castroviejo is one of the most interesting and intelligent people I know. A veteran market insider, Christopher has taught me much about the inner workings of Wall Street and the markets. We've given hundreds of financial training sessions together, taught thousands, and worked in the hedge fund world together. Christopher is a true friend and we continue to talk about the markets every day.

I have admired Marc Chaikin's work for decades. Marc is an incredible thinker and student of the markets. He's been a good friend for decades. And I still learn from him every single time we talk.

Brad Martin was a floor trader in Chicago for 20 years. He teamed up with me to design and teach trading seminars for half a dozen years. He shared much of what he knows with me about how floor trading works, about short-term trading, and was a naturally gifted teacher for our students.

Dr. Chris Szymanski helped me write through a section of the book that we ending up saving for later publication. Chris is a caring friend who is a fine trader and top-notch thinker.

All of us involved in the project would like to thank Tula Weis at John Wiley & Sons and her team for their wonderful help. Tula has been the steady, guiding hand throughout this project.

Unlike the lawns I mowed as a teen, the process of writing a book doesn't always play out in straight lines. But there's still that same great feeling of achievement when the job is done. Especially when you know there was such a wonderful team effort to get here.

—D.R.B., Jr.

PROLOGUE

I t was March 27, 1988—Palm Sunday, in fact. I was watching the sun rise from the very top of an 80-foot chemical distillation tower in one of the world's largest industrial complexes.

And I was unwinding.

You see, I'd been working at the South Carolina site for almost 24 hours—the white-collar version of a college all-nighter. The team I headed had been finalizing the startup of a facility known technically as a "continuous uranium de-nitrator." The plant, built to prepare spent uranium for long-term storage, would be the first of its type in the United States.

For an engineer like me, it was a fascinating project to get to lead.

And a demanding one, too.

For months, team members and I had been running through a comprehensive startup checklist. The dangers of processing multiple deadly materials had been accounted for and controlled. Every switch, valve, and control loop was tested and retested.

But with a plant startup like this one, there's a defining moment—a climax, if you will—when the rehearsals must end. Someone must push the button so that the facility's live performances can begin.

That's when you find out if all your hard work—and the care you put into the risk-reducing checks and rechecks—has paid off.

When you're working with radioactive materials, as we were, those efforts, and this final moment, are critically important.

Here's one example. Before the plant went live, we could actually work on the equipment wearing a minimum of protective gear. But once uranium entered the pipes, the system was "hot"—meaning it was actually radioactive. From that moment on, even simple tweaks to the system required us to don full protective gear ... and to use a much more elaborate safety plan.

For us, that first live performance had started before dawn on Palm Sunday in 1988.

I was the one who had the responsibility to push the button (hit the "Enter" key on the control system keyboard).

I can still see it all in my memory: circuits closed. Valves opened. Pumps started. The sophisticated chemical plant awoke from its startup slumber, came to life, and ran like the well-oiled machine we'd designed it to be.

Without a single hitch.

All of the startup team's hard work, all of the systematic checks and rechecks paid off. By every metric, the project was a success.

We even brought it in on time and under budget.

It was quite an achievement ... and I was understandably proud of what our team had accomplished.

But hours later, as I'd perched atop that distillation tower and watched the light come up, I remember thinking—for the first time ever—that I wanted to be something *other* than a chemical engineer.

I was physically exhausted and mentally drained (100-hour work weeks will do that to you). I was 600 miles from my lovely and talented wife. And we hadn't started our family (a biological impossibility when both spouses are in two different places).

With this project now receding in my professional rearview mirror, I realized that I was already thinking about the next phase of my career ... and my life.

With the benefit of hindsight, I now see that my high vantage point on that March morning gave me more than just a great view of daybreak.

It also allowed me to look into the future . . . my future . . . and the new professional course that ultimately led to this book.

I should tell you that by this point in my life I'd already been actively trading and investing in the financial markets for two years. I'd made some interesting discoveries. And I'd begun to understand the obstacles individual investors faced in their quest to trade effectively, safely, and profitably. (Take the area of information, for one example. I'd seen the paucity of data available to retail investors, and had seen that the little bit of information that was available was tough to understand—or just wrong.)

As an engineer, I'd spent years distilling sophisticated chemical processes into simple systems—with simple instructions—that anyone we hired and trained could follow. And I'd built in risk-management controls that let those same workers operate safely.

As I relaxed at the top of that tower that Sunday morning, I realized I could take that same simplicity, clarity, and safety and apply it to the complex and off-putting world of investing.

In other words, the same "keep-it-simple/keep-it-safe" approach that made it possible for a plant to churn out a stream of badly needed chemicals could also be used to create a system that would churn out a stream of profits, and wealth, for individual investors. And thanks to the easy-to-follow instructions—and attention to risk-minimization—the system in each of the two worlds (chemicals and investments) could be monitored and optimized in very small chunks of time.

The 10-Minute Millionaire is the result of that March 1988 epiphany.

After I climbed down from that distillation column, I spent the next 10 years straddling both worlds. I stayed with DuPont until 1999. I was the team leader and ultimate "push-the-button" guy for yet another startup, a project that also came off without a hitch—even though it posed even greater potential dangers and risks than the project I described earlier.

Having paid my dues on projects out in the field, I moved into a business-development role in a newly created DuPont-owned venture—an idea incubator designed to hatch new products, including cutting-edge fibers and composite materials.

However, even as I worked on these projects, I became more and more immersed in the investing world—learning from and trading alongside some great financial minds as I refined my own systematic approach to the financial markets.

By 1999, I was able to take early retirement from DuPont—and devote my full attention to trading and investing.

When doing something that you're passionate about, time really does fly.

Since breaking out on my own, I've co-founded two different financial-seminar and trader-coaching companies. I co-authored the book *Safe Strategies for Financial Freedom*—a *New York Times* and *Wall Street Journal* best-seller. I served as the risk-management and chief operating officer (COO) for a hedge fund. I also launched and ran three separate investing newsletters.

I've also done a fair bit of coaching, an activity that—believe it or not—really aided my quest to design a wealth-building trading system that is simple, fast, and safe.

In addition to those extracurricular pursuits, I've spent the better part of the last 16 years preparing lesson plans to help young people understand complex subjects.

For example, I've taught investing—stocks, bonds, and the financial markets—to elementary school students. I've also taught economics to kids in grades three through six to help them get ready for a statewide competition. (More than a dozen of the teams that I trained across all four of those grade levels have scored first-place finishes.)

Here, yet again, I saw how this ability to transform the most-sophisticated concepts into simple-to-follow systems led to pay dirt. Let's face it, you can't fudge "marginal utility," "opportunity costs," or "supply/demand equilibrium curves" to third graders. They either get it—and win ribbons—or they don't.

I'm proud to say that the kids I've worked with—all of them wonderful—have managed to get it.

Helping investors get it is what *The 10-Minute Millionaire* is all about. The "it" here is our system—one designed to be a reliable and repeatable way to identify and profit from the stock market extremes that show up virtually every day. By using this system, you'll have the opportunity to take a small, underperforming part of your portfolio and grow your trading account to a million dollars or more. And you'll be able to do this with consistently small commitments of time.

I've broken this book into three sections, each with a specific goal—a format designed to help you learn the 10-Minute Millionaire system in the most efficient way possible.

- Section I instills the 10-Minute Millionaire mindset. It shows you the importance of time, and how to transform it from an enemy into an ally. It presents the most useful and simple way to understand the stock market—as a big auction in which lots of items (individual stocks) are up for bid each day. And it shows you that the best markets to exploit are those experiencing out-of-whack extremes.

- Section II takes you from the mindset of the millionaire-to-be to the system that will get you there. Here we learn the benefits of a systematic approach and how the system helps us overcome the biases that can trip up traders. That's followed by the nuts and bolts of how to Find the Extreme, Frame the Trade, and Book the Profit.

- And, finally, Section III reinforces the lessons we've learned by presenting sample trades that show the system at work and reiterating key terms you'll need to keep in mind. We bolster the importance of being systematic by presenting a customized worksheet that will let you record the key elements of your trades, and we complete your training by highlighting the key points one final time.

I believe you'll enjoy the simplicity, time efficiency, and comprehensive nature of the 10-Minute Millionaire method. In fact, I hope this book serves as the life-changer I've intended it to be . . . that it allows you to look down from a higher vantage point . . . and picture a future that's financed by wealth and marked by great personal fulfillment.

After all, you deserve it.

My personal goal here is as powerful as it is simple. I want the work we do here together to give you the money and free time you need to do the things you love and help those who need you the most.

If today serves as the starting point for that new journey, that new direction in your life . . . then I'll know I succeeded.

Because you'll have succeeded, too.

—D. R. Barton, Jr.
Newark, Delaware
Fall 2016

SECTION I

It's Time to Think Like a Millionaire (aka "The Path to Wealth Is a Lot Shorter Than You Think")

INTRODUCTION

The Huck Stops Here

Study the past if you would define the future.

—Confucius

One of the most powerful lessons I learned during my career as an entrepreneur, chemical engineer, futures trader, hedge fund risk management officer, best-selling author, and TV stock analyst is also one of the simplest.

The lesson: there's nothing better than a good story to get your audience engaged.

And I've got a great tale to share with you.

The story is about the American Revolution.

And 10 minutes that changed the world.

As anecdotes go, this one's a stunner.

The lesson we learn will serve as the cornerstone for this book . . . and will end up being your ticket to a much wealthier, more fulfilling life.

So let's get started . . .

Flying South

It was 1780, and the War of Independence was in its fifth year.

Great Britain's inability to bring the rebel colonists to heel—coupled with the Redcoat defeat at Saratoga and worries that the French would throw in with the colonists—caused the Crown to shift its strategy.

To the south.

When British strategists looked at those southern colonies, they saw Loyalist strongholds and envisioned a postwar future in which agricultural products like tobacco, rice, and indigo would let them line their pockets.

At first, the southern strategy went well for the Crown.

Indeed, it went very well.

The British captured Savannah, giving them the Georgia coast. On May 12, 1780—after laying siege to Charleston, South Carolina, for about six weeks—that port city fell. And 5,000 Continental Army troops under the command of Major General Benjamin Lincoln had to surrender. It was a *humiliating* defeat—indeed, the worst loss the Americans would suffer during the whole war.

Further defeats followed: damaging losses at the Waxhaws, Camden, and Fishing Creek obliterated most of the Continental Army—leaving Great Britain with almost total control of both Georgia and South Carolina.

But instead of just holding and policing this territory, these victories emboldened the Redcoats: certain regiments of the British Army decided to inflict as much suffering as possible. Colonial morale was about as low as could be, so these particular Redcoats figured they'd rub out any remaining Patriot dissent—and maybe even get the colonists to switch sides to the soon-to-be victorious Crown.

Raids, murders, and reprisals became standard fare. Plantations were leveled, crops destroyed, and businesses wiped away. If you ever saw the Mel Gibson movie *The Patriot,* you can picture the very kind of brutality I'm talking about here.

In a rural area just outside of what's now York County, South Carolina, a man named William Hill experienced this onslaught in a very personal way.

Today, we'd refer to Hill as an entrepreneur or a self-made man. Back then, however, Hill was a pioneering "iron master." He and his partner, Isaac Hayne, constructed a massive metal works along Allison's

Creek in York County. The venture made farm implements, blacksmith tools, kitchenware, cannons, and cannonballs.

In fact, most of the cannonballs used in the siege of Charleston came from Hill's furnaces—which the colonists, not surprisingly, tried very hard to protect.

Unsuccessfully.

In June 1780, the British burned the ironworks. Hill lost his house, grain mills, saw mills, tenant houses, and 90 tenants.

Hill also lost his partner. Not long after, the British decreed that Hayne had "broken parole"—and hanged him.[1]

Force 10 from Brattonsville

The perpetrators of much of this mayhem were a troop of British light cavalry commanded by Captain Christian Huck. Huck was a Pennsylvania Loyalist and Philadelphia lawyer whose property had been confiscated after the British evacuation of that city. He was actually banished from the Keystone State, and made his way to New York, where he joined the British Army.[2]

Now Huck was operating in South Carolina. And historians like biographer Michael C. Scoggins say he had a particular hatred for the Scotch-Irish Presbyterians who made up a lot of the populace in that region's backcountry.[3] Most of those colonists were Whigs—what the British contemptuously referred to as "rebels"—and Captain Huck took great pleasure in the abuse, destruction, and death his troops engaged in. Indeed, it was his group that leveled Hill's ironworks—and burned his home.

On the night of July 11, 1780, near what is now the town of Brattonsville, South Carolina, the same William Hill we've been talking about found himself spending the night out in the open...under the stars.

It was hot. And muggy. And Hill was worried—scared even—wondering what the morning would bring.

At least, he thought, his family was safe. After losing his home, Hill stashed his family in the nearby log hut of a friendly neighbor.

And waited for dawn.

Just before first light, Captain William Hill and his ragtag band of local militia heard the first rustlings of Christian Huck's New York

Volunteers stirring from their overnight encampment. Surrounding the enemy with the stealth of practiced deer stalkers, Hill and his band of guerrilla warriors waited patiently. When the sun finally appeared over a nearby plantation, the Patriots opened fire.

And unleashed havoc.

The Redcoats—trained to fight in regimented, disciplined formations and to shoot in massed volleys—fell into chaos. Their clumsy smoothbore muskets were no match for the colonists' frontier rifles. Firing with pinpoint accuracy from behind fence cover, these Colonial farmers and woodsmen rejected the order of eighteenth-century warfare and chopped their well-trained adversaries to pieces.

For the Revolutionaries, the gains were enormous and losses slight. Dozens of enemy soldiers lay dead on the field. That included their sadistic leader, Captain Huck, who'd been felled by a headshot as he was mounting his horse to rally his troops. The Redcoats who weren't killed or wounded either surrendered or tried to flee.

Of Huck's troopers—roughly 35 dragoons, 20 New York Volunteers, and 60 Loyalist militiamen—only 24 escaped.

The Americans—150 strong at the outset—lost just one man.

But here's the best part of all.

The total time of the battle—from first shot to decisive victory—was a *mere 10 minutes*.[4]

Ten minutes.

And that 10-minute span changed the world.

That's not hyperbole.

Historians now refer to this 10-minute skirmish as "The Battle of Huck's Defeat." South Carolina historian Walter Edgar wrote that Huck's Defeat was "a major turning point in the American Revolution in South Carolina."[5] It was the first of more than 35 key battles in that state that took place in late 1780 and early 1781—all but five of which were Patriot victories.

This streak of victories in smaller battles ended up being a critical contributor to later American successes at King's Mountain and Cowpens.

Edgar said that "the entire backcountry seemed to take heart. Frontier militia had defeated soldiers of the feared British Legion." One key result: the militia brigade of American General Thomas Sumter enjoyed a stream of badly needed volunteers.

Our friend William Hill—a key figure in this world-changing 10-minute event who survived the battle and went on to become a man of importance in the years after the American Revolution—said this short, tiny engagement "was the first check the enemy had received after the fall of Charleston, and was of greater consequence than can well be supposed from an affair of [so] small a magnitude—as it had the tendency to inspire the Americans with courage and fortitude [and] teach them that the enemy was not invincible."[6]

That's a pretty impressive statement.

But I'll say it even more clearly for you...

This single 10-minute span stopped the British juggernaut cold...and ended a dark, dark stretch for this very young nation. Those 10 minutes infused the colonists with a new energy, a new confidence, and a new belief that victory was possible...even probable. It put the Patriots back in the victory column, and kicked off a string of victories that led to America's victory in the War of Independence. And it placed this country on a trajectory that would eventually lead to the United States' emergence as a global superpower.

Ten Minutes Can Change Your World

Here's the takeaway.

If a mere 10 minutes can change world history, it can certainly do the same for you...changing your history...your future...and transforming you from wannabe to winner.

Just as that short span of time ultimately allowed an agrarian upstart to steamroll the most powerful country in the world, those same 10 minutes—properly applied—will let today's individual investors wrest their financial freedom back from that seemingly invincible monolith we know as Wall Street.

To explain what I mean, let me give you some important context.

If you've been in this business for as long as I have...talk to as many people as I have...and navigated as many unique market situations as I have...you'll make a bewildering discovery.

There are a whole lot of different trading strategies that private wealth managers, mutual fund managers, hedge fund players, activist investors, and TV pundits talk about, make references to, write about, and claim to use with great success.

And when I say "a whole lot," I'm talking about a truly mind–numbing array of supposedly successful ways of making money in stocks, bonds, options, currencies, futures, commodities—and lots of more arcane financial instruments.

I'm going to let you in on a little secret: a lot of those strategies really do work.

They really do let you make money.

And here in *The 10-Minute Millionaire,* I'm not saying otherwise.

Indeed, during my trading days, I've used many of these other strategies myself.

So I'm not telling you all that there's only one way to make money. I'm not claiming that the 10-Minute Millionaire system is the only way to achieve meaningful wealth.

But what I am saying is that—out of all these systems... out of all these strategies—the approach I'm about to teach you here is the simplest, the easiest to understand and execute, and is the one that you're most likely to stick with.

And that means it's the system that's the most likely of all succeed by making you wealthy.

Because once you learn it, set it up, practice it, and allow it to run, you'll be able to maintain it in 10-minute increments.

With my strategy, those 10 minutes—employed at regular intervals, can and will:

- Halt your financial bleeding...
- Thwart the financial "enemies"—Wall Street, the taxman, and the "regulatory cesspool" we know as Washington—that threaten the well-being of your family.
- Neutralize the external geopolitical, economic, and financial market events that have obliterated lifetimes of hard work, sacrifice, and disciplined saving that so many Americans have engaged in.
- Restore your financial confidence so that you again feel compelled to pursue your personal dreams.
- And put you on a path that will end with your becoming a superpower—a financial superpower... a millionaire... a 10-Minute Millionaire.

To achieve this, you need to be like the colonists—and embrace a strategy that's guerrilla-like in both focus and execution. Indeed, the parallels between then and now are truly striking.

Wall Street is so much like the British Army of Revolutionary War vintage—almost rigid in its discipline and unable to deviate from its long-held practices. Indeed, some of Wall Street is very much like Huck's band of Loyalist raiders—gleefully targeting Main Street investors . . . to strip them of their hard-earned savings.

All of this leaves Wall Street open for attack by investors who are willing to think and act independently . . . just as the colonists successfully did. These realities create opportunities—some small and fleeting, others large and resolute . . . all of them profitable—that you can exploit.

And with the easy-to-use tools and strategies I'm going to share, you can do all of this . . . in increments as small as 10 minutes a day.

That's what *The 10-Minute Millionaire* is all about . . . taking and using that time . . . and combining it with a trading strategy that positions you for one decisive investment victory after another—with overall victory as the goal.

In this case, I'm defining victory as financial independence—millionaire status.

And with this book, I'm going to show you just how get there.

I'm going to show you a system that will let you become a true market millionaire.

And you can achieve this goal by employing my simple-to-use system in a series of 10-minute increments.

We'll start by instilling in you a 10-Minute Millionaire's mindset.

All you need to do is run the system I'll reveal in pages ahead. I've already done all the hard work—all the discovery, and all the testing—for you.

This is a money machine, plain and simple. Just keep turning the crank, and a steady stream of winning trades, and growing wealth, will pour from it.

The system that I've created is so simple I've taught it to sixth graders.

Once you learn it, it takes a mere 10 minutes a day to run.

That's it.

Set it up in the morning, then walk away and forget about it. Go to work. Take your kids to school. Hit the gym.

The 10-Minute Millionaire system will keep running in the background—generating profits beyond compare.

This isn't an algorithmic "black box." It's not "robo-trading."

What I've done here is design a system that still requires personal involvement...that still requires commitment...that still requires execution.

But it squeezes out emotion...filters out the noise...jams down the risk...and maximizes the potential for profits.

The bottom line: the 10-Minute Millionaire system puts probability on your side.

A Blueprint for Wealth

It's based on a simple set of reliable, repeatable precepts that anyone can use.

Those precepts were shaped by the decades I've spent in the capital markets, in a crucible of hard work, occasional mistakes, and occasional epiphanies.

And it all starts with one truism: financial markets run to "extremes."

That's true of broad indexes...business sectors...geographic markets...stocks and bonds...classes of assets...metals like gold...commodities like oil...and even arcane derivative instruments that the most-sophisticated institutional players use.

Markets are made up of people...meaning they're also a compilation of emotions...of fear...of greed...of predispositions...of likes and dislikes.

And because emotions govern markets, they have a tendency to overrun at tops and overrun at bottoms. That's because investors become irrationally exuberant at investment peaks and completely desolate at investment bottoms.

And you can exploit those extremes for hefty profits...often at risk levels that are well below normal.

Once you understand this simple fact, the charts of stocks, bonds, options, commodities...are as rich in what they tell you as the greatest classics in literature.

These extremes show up every single day.

They show up in broad indexes—in the Dow Jones Industrial Average and in those that represent geographic markets like Europe and Asia. They show up in specific market sectors like energy and technology. They show up in asset classes like real estate and precious metals. They show up in stocks and bonds. And these extremes are even reflected in derivative investments—those based on the underlying asset—meaning you can play these extremes in options and futures.

This reality opens up a plethora of profit opportunities—on the long side and the short side.

When markets, indexes, or asset classes are irrationally exuberant—and you catch the right signals from my system—you can bet the other way and profit on the eventual decline. Conversely, when desolation rules the roost, you can go long and profit on the rebound rally.

My system is open to all of these trading possibilities.

The 10-Minute Millionaire is designed to be a repeatable and reliable system to find and profit from the extremes in markets that happen almost every day. By using this system—even if you start by applying it to underperforming slice of your portfolio as small as $2,500—you'll have the chance to grow your trading account to a million dollars or more. And you'll do so with very small commitments of time.

Exposing the underlying principles that will let you exploit these extremes—and teaching you the setup so that you can operate this remarkable moneymaking machine on your own—comes down to a three-step program:

Step No. 1: Find the Extreme. It all starts with a signal. I'll show how to identify when a particular opportunity is out of whack—has achieved an extreme—and the precise moment when the odds of initiating a profitable trade are overwhelmingly in your favor. These conditions are rare enough to require patience and discretion, but they're also frequent enough for us to book regular profits. When we have that signal, we know it's time to attack.

Step No. 2: Frame the Trade. Next, I'll teach you exactly how to set up the trade for maximum Edge—just like a Minuteman ambush—to make a killer profit on a big price movement from behind protective cover with a well-planned escape route.

Step No. 3: Book the Profit. Finally, I'll demonstrate exactly when to take your profits, escape the scene, and move on to your next trade.

Instead of scrounging for every last penny waiting for the market to catch you off guard, you'll be miles away, already setting up your next profitable trading opportunity.

It's why this system allows for maximum profits at the minimum possible risk.

Then we'll do it all over again. Day after day, week after week.

And always 10 minutes at a time.

Follow me...follow my system—and together we'll watch your wealth mount.

At its core, the 10-Minute Millionaire isn't *just* a trading system.

It isn't just a pathway to wealth.

It's a way of life...a belief system...an actual mindset—and it's one that will allow you to live a much fuller life than you'll ever have.

Let's take a look.

Notes

1. Harry M. Ward, *Going Down Hill: Legacies of the American Revolutionary War* (New York: St. Martin's Press, 1995).

2. Michael C. Scoggins, *The Day It Rained Militia: Huck's Defeat and the Revolution in the South Carolina Backcountry, May-June 1780* (Charleston SC: History Press, 2005).

3. Ibid.

4. Culture and Heritage Museums of York County, South Carolina (chmuseums .org), "The Battle of Huck's Defeat."

5. Walter Edgar, *Partisans and Redcoats: The Southern Conflict That Turned the Tide of the American Revolution* (New York: HarperCollins, 2001).

6. William Hill, *Colonel William Hill's Memoirs of the Revolution*, 1921, edited by A. S. Salley Jr., secretary of the Historical Commission of South Carolina.

CHAPTER 1

The Critical Secret I Learned from the World's Billionaires

Lost time is never found again.

—Benjamin Franklin

I t's one of my favorite personal stories. And folks just can't seem to get enough of this tale. But the personal experience I'm about to relate also taught me some very valuable lessons, which I'm now going to share with you.

This story goes back to my days as an entrepreneur, when I was running a venture that designed, built, and installed water-desalination systems.

One of my first customers was Richard Branson.

Yes...that Richard Branson...the man so often referred to as "Billionaire Richard Branson" in media reports that I'm betting many folks think "Billionaire" is his first name.

Actually, it's Sir Richard Branson. And with my little quip, absolutely no disrespect was intended.

In fact, Richard Branson is a gentleman for whom I have great respect. Because he's one of the first people to really help me understand the value of time.

Time as a key ingredient—or raw material—of wealth.

Let me show you what I mean...

From Castaways to Kings

The British investor, philanthropist, and entrepreneur is probably best-known as the founder and builder of Virgin Group, a holding company for more than 400 ventures. And one reason Branson has been so successful is that he started early.

At 16, in fact, with a magazine called *Student*.

By the time he was 20, Branson had set up a mail-order business and—two years later—he opened a chain of record stores called Virgin Records. Throughout the 1980s, he expanded the Virgin Records music label, the Virgin Atlantic Airways Ltd. carrier, and a host of other ventures.

In July 2015, *Forbes* estimated Branson's net worth at $5.2 billion.

My interaction with Branson's entrepreneurial efforts had to do with the billionaire's private getaway, called Necker Island.

The 74-acre tract in the British Virgin Islands is wholly owned by Branson, and is part of the Virgin Ltd. Edition portfolio of high-end properties. The entire island is set up as a resort, has two private beaches, can accommodate up to 28 guests and rents out for $65,000 a day (or about $2,200 a person).

It wasn't always a resort.

Back in 1965, in fact, *Daily Telegraph* reporter Andrew Alexander and photographer Don McCullin were sent to what was then a desert island" for a castaway adventure the British newspaper hoped would last for three weeks.

The duo managed to stick it out for 14 days.

As McCullin would later say, Necker was "inhabited by snakes, scorpions, and tarantulas . . . the mosquitos and other insects were more venomous and persistent than any I had encountered in Vietnam or the Congo."

In the early-morning hours of that fifteenth day—suffering from "gathering weakness . . . out of temper and out of water," McCullin said he and his photographer colleague "hoisted the red flag and were taken off the island."

A bit more than a dozen years later, the then-28-year-old Branson learned that some of the islands in the BVI chain were for sale. He visited, and immediately realized how great they could be for putting up his record label's top stars—so he investigated a purchase. Branson and his team were given a luxury villa on one of the islands, toured several others by helicopter, and saw Necker last of all.

From the island's highest point, Branson took in the stunning view and wondrous array of wildlife—and immediately offered $100,000 for an island whose asking price was $6 million (his cash was low at that point in his entrepreneurial career).

Branson wasn't just turned down . . . he was evicted.

"The Realtor closed in on me to make the sale and said Necker Island could be all mine for the small price of around $6 million," Branson said in a recent humor-laced recollection of that time. "I considered for a moment and then made the highest offer I could, based on my available funds: $100,000. The music stopped instantly. We were taken back and unceremoniously dumped on the main island. The helicopter disappeared, the champagne evaporated, and we were left to find our own way back to New York."

Not long after, however, the island's owner—needing cash—accepted a revised offer of $180,000.

But there was a state-imposed proviso: Branson had to develop a resort within five years—or the island's ownership reverted to the state. The businessman didn't worry about that: he committed to the purchase—and then committed to creating his dream resort.

Three years and about $10 million afterward, Branson had his private resort. And as anyone can easily see, it's breathtaking. The architect combined local stone with Brazilian hardwoods for construction of a

10-bedroom villa on a hill overlooking the beach. Antiques from Asia, furniture from Bali, and rugs from India highlight the getaway. Open walls give 360-degree views and the most wondrous of soothing breezes. That brings us back to my story.

Learning in Luxury

In the late 1990s, my company constructed the desalination facility that I talked about a moment ago. In my own telling of this tale, I like to tell listeners that when they read about Beyoncé, Oprah, or Robert De Niro staying on that island, they're reading about celebrities... drinking my water.

That quip always sparks a round of laughter.

But I also share this little factoid.

At $65,000 a day, the whole cost of constructing this resort could be recouped in just five months.

All thanks to the shrewdness, patience, vision, and personal financial control that Branson displayed—even as a 28-year-old entrepreneur.

Indeed, there are the "Five Lessons of Necker Island" that, put to use, will help make you a successful investor:

- Necker Island Lesson Number 1: Have a Plan—and Act on That Plan. Branson had a plan... He wanted to create a private luxury getaway. He did the legwork, he identified his investment target, and he made his move.
- Necker Island Lesson Number 2: Look for Bargains. Granted, paying $180,000 for an island worth $6 million is an extreme example of a bargain. But in real estate, in stocks, and in other parts of the financial and capital asset markets, bargains come along more often than you'd think. You have to be patient. You have to understand what you're buying. And you have to be ready to act when you spot one.
- Necker Island Lesson Number 3: Invest Within Your Means. At that point in his entrepreneurial career, Branson knew what he could afford to invest. As much as he loved Necker Island, and understood its potential, he also knew his outlay limit. So he refused to over-pay... even after his champagne had been taken away and he'd been evicted during his investigative trip.

- Necker Island Lesson Number 4: When You Finally Do Make Your Move, Be Decisive. Once the seller took his offers seriously, Branson made his move. And he embarked on the project and got it done well within the five-year deadline he faced.

If you're one of those folks with a wonderful eye for detail, you notice there were only four lessons listed—even though I promised five.

And, indeed, there is a fifth.

And it's the most important lesson of all.

Like capital, *time* is a valuable resource.

That, in fact, is Necker Island Lesson Number 5: Time Is the Single-Most-Valuable Resource Investors Have.

Used correctly, time is our most powerful ally.

Used incorrectly—or ignored outright—time is our biggest enemy.

It's not enough to merely acknowledge this lesson.

You actually have to embrace it . . . as a mindset . . .

The fact is that this lesson is the central element of the wealth system I'm going to teach you during the rest of this book.

It's time for you to embrace—as your own—what I refer to as the 10-Minute Millionaire mindset.

Let me start by showing it to you . . .

That Ticking Sound You Hear...

Ten minutes . . . it's a time interval we've already talked quite a bit about—despite having just met.

And yet . . . it's an interval of time that most of us fritter away without a second thought.

We'll waste it watching a TV show we have absolutely no interest in.

We'll waste it surfing the Net . . . jumping from one link to the next on the mindless trivia shrewd e-commerce marketers refer to as *clickbait*.

We'll waste it daydreaming . . . about nothing in particular.

We listen as those ticks of the clock run off—indeed, disappear—without a single pang of regret.

But what if I told you that with each 10-minute interval you waste, you're potentially flushing away $1,000, $10,000, or even $100,000?

Properly directed—properly focused—those minutes... those ticks of the clock... could each add hundreds, thousands, or hundreds of thousands of dollars to your net worth.

Indeed, over time, those ticks of the clock could add... millions.

To make my point—in fact, to illustrate this 10-Minute Millionaire mindset—let me share another story... two stories, in fact.

The first of these two tales is a favorite of investing icon Warren Buffett—the "Oracle of Omaha" and the chairman of vaunted investment vehicle Berkshire Hathaway, Inc. (NYSE: BRKA).

Years ago, in an essay titled "The Joys of Compounding," a then-32-year-old Buffett shared this story.

> I have it from unreliable sources that the cost of the voyage [Spanish Queen] Isabella originally underwrote for Columbus was approximately $30,000. This has been considered at least a moderately successful utilization of venture capital. Without attempting to evaluate the psychic income derived from finding a new hemisphere, it must be pointed out that... the whole deal was not exactly another IBM. Figured very roughly, the $30,000 invested at 4 percent compounded annually would have amounted to something like $2 trillion.[1]

Buffett makes two very important points here.

The first is about focus... about not wasting the capital that we have. And the second is about time—and the powerful ally it can be.

Translation: even trifling sums must be invested with the utmost care. To the Oracle of Omaha, wasting 30 grand represents not the loss of $30,000... but the missed opportunity to make *$2 trillion*.[2]

Wow...

And just as *money wasted now* represents a potential fortune not reaped in the future, *time* wasted now is *also* a fortune not earned.

In some ways, it's a bigger deal to waste time than it is to waste money. That's because *time* is the one commodity that you can't create more of.

After all, if you spend a dollar, you can always find another.

But once you waste a minute... or five minutes... or 10 minutes... those ticks of the clock are gone...

Forever...

There's one particular group that understands this as well as anyone. I'm talking about the builders and shapers of the world economy . . . the holders of the bulk of the wealth both here in the United States and in the top markets abroad.

I'm talking about the world's billionaires.

Richard Branson's peers.

Here's what I mean.

The Private Lives of the World's Elite

As a recent report in *Inc.* magazine underscores, this group of super-achievers fully understand that time is unrivaled as a "scarce resource." In that report, writer/entrepreneur John Rampton said he found 12 habits that the world's billionaires all seem to share.[3]

Those include such daily rituals as:

- Taking time for family: Carlos Slim Helu, number six on Forbes's list of the world's billionaires, with a current net worth of $49.5 billion, is a telecom mogul who is currently the honorary chairman of America Movil SAB de CV (NYSE ADR:AMX). He devotes his evenings to his six children and numerous grandchildren, Rampton writes. These execs may be tough as nails in the boardroom, but they see it as a gift when they're able to read to their kids or tuck them in at night.
- Taking time to exercise: Dole Food Co., Inc. Chairman David Murdock, number 231 on the Forbes 400 list, with a net worth $3.0 billion, is 93—and plans to see 125. He credits his staying power to yoga, which he does each evening. Wealthy folks spend so much time being so focused—and tightly scheduled—that they need workout time to stay sharp and fit.
- Taking time for gratitude: Finally—and perhaps most important of all—is a habit that we should all remember: be thankful for what you achieve. As Rampton writes, "Before closing their eyes for the night, an astonishing number of billionaires focus on what they feel grateful for in their lives, no matter how small it may seem." This has led many to feelings of contentment while adding a jolt of joy to

their lives. And it's not just the vast majority of billionaires that find gratitude useful—science agrees. Research from best-selling author Dr. Sonya Lyubomirsky showed that gratitude exercises, practiced regularly, improved emotional and even physical health. The bottom line? Show gratitude and improve your quality of life.

I could continue here, but I really don't need to: the pattern is clear... as is the message.

The world's richest folks—the people who know the most about wealth and what it takes to achieve it—understand that time is a scarce resource... meaning it's a resource that's not to be squandered.

Time can help you *make* a fortune. Time can help you *keep* that fortune.

And time can help you enjoy that fortune... which, after all, is the whole reason for amassing a fortune in the first place.

To me—for purposes of our 10-Minute Millionaire mindset—here's what's really fascinating.

Each of the dozen rituals Rampton wrote about is an activity that can be fulfilled in increments of 10 minutes. Some—a diary entry, for example—might be taken care of in a single 10-minute tranche.

Others—running a board meeting for a local charity—might consume multiple 10-minute increments.

Ten minutes... it's intriguing how that seemingly insignificant amount of time keeps cropping up...

In a turning-point battle in the American Revolutionary War.

In the daily lives of the world's billionaires ...

And in the rest of this book ...

With regards to these billionaires, the point to keep in mind is that these folks use their time wisely—even though they've already reached the billionaire's club.

You see, they long ago grasped the secret to investing success I want to share with you right now.

Most folks believe that *money* is the key to wealth.

And, to be sure, it's important.

Here's the thing, however ...

Money may be *a key* to meaningful wealth.

But *time*... those precious ticks of the clock that once gone can never be recouped ... is *the key*.

The wealthy investors and business leaders who I know and deal with view those minutes as a precious scarce resource, as a key to a fuller life, and as the raw materials for additional wealth.

They deploy and apportion those minutes judiciously—even shrewdly. They put those minutes to use in their business and investing pursuits. But they also use those minutes wisely at home, in their private lives . . . even just before they retire for the day and head for bed.

These habits combine to create a true formula for success.

And they also demonstrate a shared appreciation for the value of time . . . for the ticks of the clock.

If you now see and understand that simple fact—that time is a scarce commodity . . . and that time deployed in 10-minute increments can be transformed into meaningful wealth—you've embraced one of the two key building blocks of what I refer to as the 10-Minute Millionaire mindset.

And if that appreciation of time is one of those building blocks, then a deep-seated belief—that it's *absolutely possible* for you to become a millionaire—is the other.

The Basic Tenets of Prodigious Wealth

One discovery I've made through the years is that most investors view millionaire status as only a dream: they enjoy thinking about what it would be like to be wealthy—but view it as something that could never be attained.

That's the wrong way to think about it.

You see, millionaire status is actually more of a *goal*—a goal that can be worked toward and achieved, just like earning a graduate degree, buying a first house, or retiring early.

In other words, if becoming a millionaire is something you know you want to do, you establish it as a goal, put a time frame on it, and work backward to craft a plan that will get you there.

Indeed, as was illustrated by the 1996 best-seller *The Millionaire Next Door*—a seminal study of America's stealthy wealthy class—the populations of literal millionaires (households with a net worth of $1 million or more) is much bigger than most folks might think.

As authors Thomas J. Stanley and William D. Danko superbly chronicled, the nation's millionaires tend to fit a very precise profile. They spend less than they earn, and avoid status objects like super-big houses or obscenely expensive cars. And they manifest real discipline when it comes to saving and investing—and they do so over very long periods of time.

This lack of ostentation and a tendency to act and live just like "regular folks" is the reason you often don't recognize a millionaire as such when you meet them—hence the "millionaire next door" tagline.

To me, that last point—that it's not all that easy to say who's a millionaire and who isn't—is the most intriguing point of all.

Here's why.

If it's possible to meet a group of people—and not be able to tell who is a millionaire and who isn't—*then why couldn't one of the millionaires in that group be you?*

The short answer: There's no reason it can't be—as long as you believe it's possible.

And thanks to the 10-Minute Millionaire system, it is possible.

You see, in addition to the ones I've already described, there's one other trait that many "next-door millionaires" share. They are what that book's authors refer to as "Prodigious Accumulators of Wealth," or PAWs.

To be a PAW, you have to have a net worth that's higher than might seem possible, given your age and income level.

Most of that wealth is accumulated the old-fashioned way—through time, planning and discipline.

However, just because these PAWs are good savers and disciplined investors doesn't mean they aren't opportunistic.

Obviously, PAWs avoid roll-the-dice type of investments. But they will take risks if those risks are calculated, and if the underlying investment offers a high potential returns. As the authors noted, for the right opportunity PAWs will go into such financial opportunities as stocks, private equity and venture capital investments, and even financial stakes in operating businesses.

The bottom line: These PAWs *will* take financial risks—if the odds and rewards make those risks worthwhile.

If you bring together all of what we've been talking about here, it really describes the 10-Minute Millionaire system—which was designed to turn you into a "wealth accumulator."

If your goal is to become a millionaire, and you believe that goal is attainable, discipline must become a core piece of your plan. You want to be a good saver. You want to have a net worth that's high relative to your income. You want to eschew ostentation.

But you also want to become a "wealth accumulator." You want to supercharge your rate of return.

And you'll start by taking a small slice of the underperforming part of your portfolio—and using that as the seed capital for the trading strategy that I'm going to teach you in this book.

And as I detail this system, I want you to remember three key concepts—concepts that I'll flesh out with real numbers and will tie together as I teach you the 10-Minute Millionaire strategy.

First, becoming a millionaire isn't just a dream—it's a goal. And goals can be achieved if you have a plan to get you there. A plan demands discipline—which I'd define as a series of steps or a checklist you can follow. That's what a system does—it gives you those steps to follow. And the 10-Minute Millionaire system was designed with this specific goal in mind.

Second, if you string together a series of quick-but-modest (even small) gains, but you do so over a sustained stretch, the power of compounding will leave you with a *hefty* sum in a stunningly short period of time. For instance, if you can pull down a 4% gain every other week for 26 weeks, you'll *more than double* your starting capital in a single year. The reason for this is very simple: Seemingly small gains earned quickly actually work out to big, big gains when they are "compounded." So if you start out by putting $2,500 "at risk"—and you achieve the 4% win every other week that I just talked about—you'd hit the million-dollar mark in five years, 11 months. If your "at risk" capital at the outset is $10,000, then you'd hit the million-dollar threshold in four years, six months. And remember, we're just talking here about the trading portion (the "prodigious" wealth generator) slice of your overall strategy. In addition to this trading system, you're also traveling the more-conventional "save-what you earn" path to wealth.

Third, balance risk and return. I know that sounds boring—like something your insurance agent might say to you—but it's so incredibly important. It's by keeping your risk in check that you're able to string all those wins together...and reap those big annualized results. What's great about the 10-Minute Millionaire system is that all this is so simplified and systematized that you can identify the stocks you want to trade, establish your risk/return parameters, and input the actual trades in 10-minute sittings—just as the system name says.

Here's one promise I can make you. As you get into this more and more, and get more adept at screening for stocks and setting up new trades as you close out their predecessors for nice gains, you'll not only get revved up about the money you're making—you'll have fun doing it.

Indeed, from the strategy and mindset I've described to you here flows a wealth-building strategy that, once learned, will be employed over and over again. Day after day, week after week, and year after year.

Always in 10-minute increments.

Now you're ready to hear it all...

And I'm ready to share it...

Notes

1. Warren Buffett, "The Joys of Compounding" (excerpt from Buffet Partnership, Ltd.), January 18, 1963.

2. Anonymous, *The Master Money Plan* (Baltimore, MD: Money Map Press, LLC, Fall 2016).

3. John Rampton, "12 Evening Routines of Billionaires That You Need to Try," *Inc.* magazine, November 2015.

4. *The Master Money Plan.*

CHAPTER 2

Investing—The Ultimate Extreme Sport

Men, it has been well said, think in herds; it will be seen that they go mad in
herds, while they only recover their senses slowly, one by one.
                                        —Author Charles Mackay,
        Extraordinary Popular Delusions and the Madness of Crowds

Since we seem to be in a storytelling mode here, let me keep the streak going by telling another tale here – this one about the nature of the financial markets.

As someone who's been trading futures for almost 30 years . . . who's spent a decade and a half as the risk-management officer for a hedge fund . . . who's taught seminars on day trading . . . who's talked with some of the top market experts of our time in the "green rooms" while getting ready to appear as a weekly guest expert on some of the top financial shows on national television...and who's coached high-net-worth investors...I can vouch for this one simple fact: people are obsessed with making the capital markets seem as complex as possible.

Indeed, they make *such* an effort to persuade others of this complexity that they buy into it themselves.

And, in doing so, they make themselves vulnerable to the same emotion-driven miscues as everyone else.

Trust me when I tell you this: at their most basic level, financial markets are actually *very* simple beings.

They're auctions.

Huge auctions worth a lot of money—and guided by a numbing amount of technology—but auctions just the same.

My story illustrates this...and also demonstrates how emotions, biases, and imperfect information can lead an investor astray.

I've told this tale many, many times through the years. And more often than not, my listener ends up having one of the biggest investing epiphanies of their lives. (I even know when to watch for the "knowing nod" from the person I'm telling this to.)

Anatomy of an Auction Surprise

Many years ago, my church decided to run a charity auction. Everyone was encouraged to donate something of value to be auctioned off the following week—with the proceeds going toward our mission and outreach efforts. "Don't just donate your old and worn-out items," our pastor urged. "Bring some good stuff to the auction."

To further set the scene, I have to tell you that this took place long before the dawn of the smartphone. In fact, the cellphone was still a rarity.

I remember this well because we'd recently experienced problems with our old cassette-based answering machine (including the loss of an *extremely* important message). And I really, really wanted one of the new digital models. When the AT&T model 1337 debuted, it was the very first digital unit on the market—and retailed for a hefty $150. And boy, were they popular: they proved tougher to find than the first Apple iPhones and the local stores were *constantly* sold out.

But I finally found one. And I bought it.

Naturally, at precisely the same time, my dad found one down in Virginia—and gave it to me as a gift.

Remembering my pastor's words about donating "good stuff" to the auction, I figured that this tough-to-find, state-of-the-art piece of technology would be an awesome auction item... perhaps even the crown jewel item of the night. (In all candor, I even had visions of it selling above purchase price because of its relative scarcity.)

When auction night arrived, I was looking forward to the raucous scrum of bidders emerging spontaneously from their seats when my prized donation was announced at the podium.

What I saw instead was silence.

Indifferent silence.

Nobody who came to that charity auction seemed the least bit interested in this latest-and-greatest technological marvel.

The bidders this day weren't tech geeks like me. They didn't care a whit about the real value of my donated digital marvel.

The auctioneer started the bidding at $15—just 10 percent of the store price.

No bites.

"How about $12, who'll give me $12? $10?"

And the offer price kept dropping. I think the machine ended up selling for maybe two bucks. And for all I know, that may have just been a "sympathy bid."

As I watched this painful episode, I realized that I was learning a valuable lesson about the nature of auctions... and markets.

What I didn't realize, however, was that my learning opportunity had a second tranche. A second part.

A bit later that evening, while I was still trying to figure out what had happened, a rusty hand-trowel for gardening came up for bid. Far from being some of the "good stuff" our pastor had implored us to bring, this item looked like something a guy grabbed from the floor of his garage (or his trash can) as he walked out the door so that he didn't arrive at the auction empty-handed.

Now I enjoy a homegrown beefsteak tomato as much as the next person, so in the spirit of the auction, I opened the bidding at about half of what a new trowel would cost.

I was immediately trumped by the woman in front of me...and her bid was just as quickly left in the rearview mirror by yet another bidder.

I watched...with equal parts shock and awe...as the bidding for this rusty/crusty garden implement spiraled skyward faster than a share of Netscape on the morning of its dot-com-era dawning IPO.

In fact, to my utter astonishment, the bidding for this oxidized piece of hardware was soon double the price of a new one—and it kept going from there.

When the bidding was finally over (I looked around...literally expecting to see smoke clearing), I realized that I *had* to have answers. I sought out the winner...and asked why he'd been willing to bid so high.

His answer was intriguing, for it was a combination of "perceived value" and "heat of the moment" emotion. He explained that this was an old-style trowel...one constructed with a much-heavier gauge metal than any you'd find in stores now. But he also sheepishly confessed that he'd been swept up in the excitement of the auction, and had bid more than he intended...and probably more than it was worth.

The result: crazy high bidding for a rusty old trowel (and a gaveled price that was many times what my "real value" $150 answering machine actually fetched, I must add).

The similarities between auctions and markets were really drilled into my head that evening ...

It didn't matter what *I* thought something was worth. The *market* would decide the price. And sometimes the market drives prices to extremes—levels much higher or much lower than we believe is warranted.

I drove home that evening understanding just how much this simple charity auction reflected the actual operation of global financial markets.

Most items at the auction sold about where you or I would guess—at a reasonable price, but not at a ridiculously low price. That's because most people knew the value of the items and if one of them was "trading" at too low a price, another bidder would step in and offer a little more, knowing they'd still get it for a good price. This would keep going until the item was reasonably priced—except, of course, for the few times when people got crazy.

One of those instances was with my answering machine—since nobody at this particular auction understood it well enough to pay its estimated value. That resulted in a price that, in essence, was a market "extreme."

The rusty trowel represented an extreme at the other end of the emotional spectrum. With the garden tool, there were many, many folks who were interested and willing to pay up for the chance to take it home. The result: the "market" for that garden tool overran—in a big way—to the upside.

Empirically valuable assets shouldn't sell for pennies on the dollar. Rusty metal shouldn't command premium prices—even in a small, private auction of a few hundred folks. But at live physical auctions—as well as in financial-market auctions—people get crazy. And when people get crazy, prices move to extremes—over and over again.

That's the very real nature of auction markets... they're a compilation of lots and lots of people—each of them making the bids and the offers. And people are human... and are governed by emotions. They're not *Star Trek* Vulcans... who are guided by pure logic.

Human beings have emotions and psychological biases that logic simply can't account for.

Importantly for us, these qualities manifest themselves as market extremes—and they show up all the time in the broad indexes, in individual stocks and bonds, in sectors—and even in physical assets like gold or real estate.

The markets get stretched and pulled by human psychology and then often snap back in spectacular fashion. Once we learn to recognize these extreme conditions, we can consistently profit from them.

I'm going to show you how...

Those Inefficient "Efficient Markets"

On the morning of January 19, 1977, veteran radio disk jockey Rick Shaw glanced out of the window of his station at WAXY-106 and blinked in disbelief. White flakes drifted lazily down from an overcast sky... blanketing Fort Lauderdale beach with a light dusting of snow. After a split second of stunned hesitation, he ran back to the broadcast booth, pulled out a dusty vinyl LP, and put on Bing Crosby's *White Christmas* (much to the confusion of his windowless listeners across

Broward County, Florida). The *Miami News* headline that afternoon blared, "Snow in Miami!" as area-wide temperatures plummeted into the mid-20s.

Like most of us, Shaw didn't need a PhD in meteorology or an IQ of 180 to immediately grasp that snow flurries in Miami constituted an extreme weather event. If he had been able to buy, say, temperature futures that profited if the mercury rose above freezing over the next few days, he surely would have made a fortune.

We all know that extreme events are rare—and usually short-lived. A fluke convergence of two arctic cold fronts may pull temperatures down to their frigid limits temporarily, but they're sure to snap back to normal once the weather system passes.

Experiencing a snowstorm in Miami is certainly a unique—even extreme—event. But how do we know what constitutes an extreme in the stock market? Prices jump all over the place—seemingly for all sorts of reasons. Unlike my charity auction, we don't have the luxury of tapping a hedge fund manager on the shoulder and asking: "Excuse me, madam, could you please explain why you paid so much for that biotech company with no earnings?"

And that's the challenge. Even if we could drink from the fire hose of information and make sense of it all, how can we look at a stock price and tell whether it's a good deal or a total rip-off?

According to the vaunted "Efficient Markets Hypothesis," or EMH, you don't need to. The EMH says there are no extremes and no exploitable opportunities—meaning you have no opportunity to earn what Wall Streeters like to refer to as an "outsized profit."

At every point in time, the price of a share of stock is the fair value between what buyers are willing to pay (the bid) and sellers are willing to accept (the ask) based on a complete and instantaneous understanding of all available information. If you do somehow manage to beat the markets, it's purely due to chance.

This idea of perfectly efficient markets gained enthusiastic traction among academics in the early 1970s and earned even wider popularity with the publication of Burton G. Malkiel's seminal book, *A Random Walk Down Wall Street*. The average Woodstock hippie was at no greater advantage or disadvantage in the markets than a suit-clad Wall Street pro. Even better, it permitted ivory-towered theorists who had never risked their own money in the market to attribute any success of the real-world stock-picking practitioners to blind luck rather than intellectual skill.

Since the 1970s, the theory of unbeatable markets has been preached to generations of MBA-seekers and Main Street retail investors as absolute truth (mostly by the vested interests of index fund companies and fee-based financial advisors selling asset allocation services). "Buy-and-hold" became the mantra for a generation of investors.

Eventually, however, bird-dogging researchers began to find cracks in the foundation of the EMH.

And over time, those cracks have widened... a lot.

In the late 1970s Professor Sanjoy Basu found that value stocks— stocks with low-price/earnings (P/E) ratios—earned consistently higher risk-adjusted returns compared to both the overall market and their high-P/E peers. A few years later, Donald Keim proved that small company stocks also repeatedly and consistently outperformed larger-company stocks, month over month, year after year.

Those findings, of course, completely contradicted the Efficient Markets Hypothesis.

Adherents found this blasphemous: after all, the EMH tells us that no basket of stocks—no matter how artfully chosen—can consistently outperform the broader index. It was starting to seem like the perfectly efficient and mechanically precise markets were somehow tainted by an irrational human element, one that overly discounted certain classes of stocks.

During the 1980s, Yale economist Robert Shiller did some Efficient Markets hypothesizing of his own.

Since the EMH holds that share prices move only in proportion to new information—and since most of that new data consisted of small, incremental changes above or below a baseline expectation (for example, an earnings revision of a penny, or a marginally reduced sales forecast)— Shiller reasoned that most daily stock price changes should also be small, infrequent, and center around a stable long-term trendline.

After testing his logic against historical market data, Shiller made a discovery that flummoxed EMH believers. Markets, he found, are *way more* volatile than the EMH could ever explain. Seemingly insignificant news events drove prices in extreme ways—and sometimes, stock prices made dramatic moves... for no clear reason at all.

Not wanting to accept such financial heresy, the EMH zealots fought back. This time they said, markets may not be perfect, but they're efficient in the sense that any anomalies are small, short-lived, and impossible to profit from. While you might get lucky sometimes, nobody can consistently outperform the markets year after year.

To bolster the argument, the Bogle Research Institute (of Jack Bogle, founder of index fund giant Vanguard) examined 355 mutual funds and found that "just" 22 beat the market by more than 1 percent every year for 30 years. In a commentary worthy of George Orwell's *1984,* Bogle himself declared the study proof that EMH is real and that actively managed funds consistently underperform the market index.

Despite Bogle's best efforts at double-speak, EMH says that *nobody* can consistently outperform the market over time. Even one excess return in 30 years would be enough to destroy EMH, but 22?

If market performance is truly random and each manager has a 50/50 chance of beating the market every year, at the end of a single decade, there would be no winners. Put another way, you would need more than 11 billion people (roughly double the world's population) repeatedly flipping coins in sequence to end up with 22 who landed heads 30 times in a row. Having 22 winners out of just 355 contestants is an astounding result that should have put the final nail in the EMH coffin.

Ghosts in the Machine

By the mid-1980s, EMH was on its back legs. A new school of thought called "Behavioral Finance" was helping harmonize the inconsistencies between theoretical models and real-world results. Blending economic analytics with human psychology, the behaviorists are finally shedding light on the true nature of the markets . . . and refuting the EMH once and for all.

In one case, researchers Werner DeBondt and Richard Thaler proved that human psychology is a major factor in how stock prices move. The two researchers proved scientifically what you and I understand intuitively: human investors overreact.

Despite knowing that they want to buy low and sell high, investors do just the opposite. They pile into the hottest stocks . . . and run them way up above their real value. And they dump stocks that are falling . . . both deepening and accelerating downtrends to the point that stocks end up trading for much, much less than they're really worth.

Further studies confirmed a whole host of psychological biases that influence the markets every day. We suffer from "optimism bias" (80 percent of motorists rate themselves as above-average drivers). We're subject to confirmation bias (once we've made a decision, we pay attention to facts that support our view and reject ones that don't). Humans are loss-averse (we hate losing more than we like winning, so we tend to take profits quickly while postponing loss-cementing sales in the hope that a "dog with fleas" stock will somehow rebound).

Regardless of how we explain and label these psychological market underpinnings, it's enough to know that they're real. We experience them all the time in the form of bubbles and crashes, irrational exuberance, and selling frenzies.

If you remain committed to the idea of efficient markets—or if you are an avowed buy-and-hold investor—I completely understand.

Just as well-meaning teachers and powerful institutions once taught folks that the sun revolves around the earth, certain seemingly simple and elegantly false theories can be tough to give up on.

But the fact that you are reading this book tells me that you're ready for a new beginning . . . for a new opportunity . . . for a new reality.

So let's start with this single simple statement.

Markets are indeed beatable.

In fact, research proves that:

- Certain classes of stocks like small caps and value stocks consistently and repeatedly beat the market (Basu, Fischer, Scholes, and Keim).
- Investors tend to overreact—meaning stocks get pushed and pulled to extremes and experience excess volatility *way beyond* what fundamental drivers like future-earnings expectations could support (Shiller, DeBondt, and Thaler).

- Dozens of investment managers—some you've heard of, most of whom you haven't—*do* outperform the markets consistently and repeatedly (Bogle).

Taken together, those disparate facts tell us that financial markets are not always efficient in the short run. Indeed, they sometimes get stretched and pulled to temporary extremes by irrational human behavior—otherwise known as *emotion*.

And we can profit from those extremes... often, in a big way.

For those of you who've taken the bold step to find out about my 10-Minute Millionaire system, there's only one important conclusion to reach.

You can win the trading game and gain the wealth you desire.

By this I mean that your achieving wealth is *completely* in the realm of possibility. It means that, despite what the academics say, you have the opportunity to get wealthy like many successful traders before you. Indeed, you have as much a right to achieve wealth as anyone else out there... as much of a right as any of the millionaires or billionaires you read about... or that we've talked about already. And you don't have to become a market monk and devote your life to trading, either. You can do it all in just *10 minutes* a day.

And you've taken the courageous—and extreme—personal step to make that possible.

That means it's now my job to help make your desire for wealth... for a fuller life... for dreams come true... a tangible reality.

So let's next understand—more specifically—how emotion helps drive share prices.

A Keynesian Game—Playing the Player, Not the Cards

To better appreciate the role of the human element in the financial markets—and how that helps create extremes—let's consider a variation of an experiment or game that builds upon a theory by legendary economist John Maynard Keynes.

In this game, participants are asked to pick a number between 1 and 100. The winner is the person who picks the number closest to two-thirds of the average of all numbers guessed. For example, let's say the contestants picked the following numbers:

Alice	Bart	Chris	Doug	Ellie	Fred	Greg	Homer	Average	2/3rds Avg.
15	28	30	43	57	74	75	79	50	33

The average of all guesses was 50, so the winner was Chris, who guessed 30—the closest guess to the number 33 (or two-thirds of the average).

Keynes surmised that participants would play the game at various levels of sophistication.

Let me show you what I mean...then I'll explain you how this applies to financial markets—and the extremes we're going to set out to exploit for gain.

Level 1 players assume the results will be evenly distributed as if by a random number generator (sort of like our preceding example). As such, the average of all numbers would be 50 and the Level 1 player would guess exactly 33 (equal to two-thirds of the average of 50).

This strategy works great if, indeed, the market was some dispassionate force (or everybody else playing was an idiot). What the Level 1 player completely forgets is that the numbers selected are picked by *other* smart human beings, each trying to out-game his or her playmates.

Level 2 players assume everyone else in the game is a Level 1 player and, therefore, the average of their picks will be 33. Hence, a Level 1 player picks 22 (or two-thirds of 33). For example:

	Level 1 Players						Level 2 Player		
Alice	Bart	Chris	Doug	Ellie	Fred	Greg	Homer	Average	2/3rds Avg.
33	33	33	33	33	33	33	23	35	23

And so it goes. Level 3 players try to out-think the Level 2 players and pick 15 and so on.

If it's starting to sound like that old vaudeville gag—the old "I know that you know that I know" shtick—well, you're starting to understand the nature of the markets we all invest in.

Taken to its extreme (which is the precise point of this chapter), an infinitely reasoned (or rational) player sees that the sequence will eventually converge to zero and would choose accordingly.

This Level Infinity player would also be the game's biggest loser:

| Level 1 | | | Level 2 | | Level 3 | | Level ∞ | | |
Alice	Bart	Chris	Doug	Ellie	Fred	Greg	Homer	Average	2/3rds Avg.
50	50	50	33	33	15	15	0	31	21

Surprise ...

Here's why that's true, however: without realizing it, this ultimate player has, in essence, gone full circle and embraced a variant of the now-discredited Efficient Markets Hypothesis. They forgot the simple fact that humans are not infinitely reasoned (or at least they don't think that others are).

In fact, real-world experiments of this type find that most people assume that market participants are thinking up to about three moves ahead. Winning guesses tend to be around 20. That's 13 points short of random markets. But it's still 20 points away from perfectly rational.

That gives us *a lot* of room to play in . . . and a lot of room in which to make *big money.*

What's remarkable to me is that this experiment in human psychology mirrors what we see in the real-world financial markets. Most people assume other traders are acting rationally most of the time (that is, Level 1). But once a trend starts, people try to outguess the other players (I know, that you know, that I know). And that leads to stocks, bonds, or entire markets getting pulled to extremes that we can exploit for big, big profits—over and over again.

On the flip side, traders don't believe that humans aren't infinitely irrational either. They know the herd will run in one direction for a few rounds of "let's out-think the other guy" . . . but that this little game will get old and scary for emotional investors—really fast.

Hence, once a price trend in the market starts, it tends to continue—sometimes for longer and further than we would ever predict (that is, an extreme).

At some point, however, this game is played out.

Traders come to their senses and stocks/bonds/markets or gold that had been enthusiastically overbought (driven up to extreme highs) or disconsolately oversold (hammered to extreme lows) finally snap back to a level that may not be perfectly efficient, but is at least less irrational than its former extreme.

Cashing in on those price extremes is the foundation of *The 10-Minute Millionaire*. And the good news is that actionable extremes come in many different sizes, shapes, and time frames.

Let's look at some concrete examples so that we can see exactly what these extremes look like.

Bubblicious Profits

When you hear the term "market extreme," the examples that first leap to mind are the notorious "bubbles" or speculative manias of history.

And that's totally understandable. After all, these are the most extreme... extremes—the instances in which investors get crazy. And these "extreme extremes" are also the best evidence that markets aren't as efficient as the EMH would have us believe.

And while bubbles do occur quite regularly (we've had two in the U.S. stock markets since 2000), we're not counting on these as part of our 10-Minute Millionaire strategy. Our goal there is to find and profit from the shorter-term extremes—the temporary out-of-whack mispricing of stocks that show up every day.

Even so, it's well worth our time to take a look at market "bubbles" (also known as "market manias" or "speculative frenzies") to give us a better understanding of the near-term extremes we'll be targeting (and profiting from) over and over again.

Bubbles are the big brother of the out-of-whack pricing extremes that we're going after—and involve an entire index, sector, asset class, or geographic market... as opposed to the single stock that we're targeting.

But the single-stock and market-bubble extremes share some common traits, which is why their charts will show a very similar price action. Just look at Figure 2.1 which depicts some of the best-known market manias of the past.

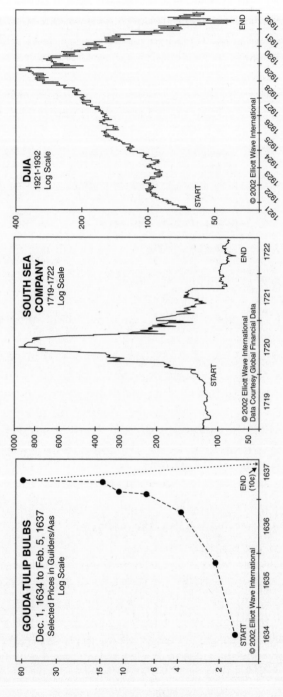

Figure 2.1 Famous Market Manias

38

While these remarkably similar trading patterns can't be explained by rational decision-making, the anthropological emotion behind them is hilariously clear as we see in Figure 2.2.

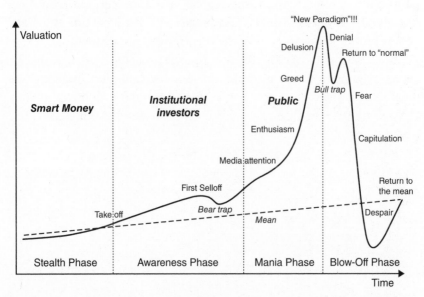

Figure 2.2 Psychology of a Stock Market Bubble
SOURCE: © Dr. Jean-Paul Rodrigue, Department of Global Studies & Geography, Hofstra University

Or, as *Psychology Today* noted in July 2011: "In stock market bubbles, human nature comes in and mucks up elegant economic theories. Even if no one believes [prices will continue to rise], as long as they believe that other people might believe it, they should start to buy it. The price goes up. They make money. It's a self-fulfilling prophecy."[1]

What Is a Bubble?

According to Nasdaq.com (a market segment that has experienced a fair share of bubbles): a bubble is a market phenomenon characterized by surges in asset prices to levels significantly above the fundamental value of that asset. Bubbles are often hard to detect in real time because there is disagreement over the fundamental value of the asset.

And don't think for a moment that bubbles are just anomalies from centuries past. We've had many serious bubbles that inflated and burst in recent years. In fact, many market observers (including me) think that bubbles are coming with greater regularity in this "new economy" era that allows us to access information faster and that lets both individual and institutional investors redeploy their money instantaneously.

Since the start of this millennium, the stock market has experienced a number of these boom-and-bust cycles—with bubbles that inflated and then burst spectacularly. Here are two bubbles in one chart in the U.S. stock market that most readers will readily recognize (see Figure 2.3).

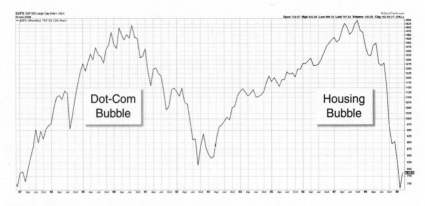

Figure 2.3   Recent Stock Market Bubbles
SOURCE: Chart courtesy of StockCharts.com

There have been other financial bubbles in recent years, too. In 2015, China's Shanghai Composite Index dropped 44.9 percent in the 11 weeks following that year's June 15 high. And while there is no shortage of extremes in the form of bubbles, we don't have to wait for such long-term craziness to set in. Since human nature is notoriously consistent through the ages, don't expect these kinds of extremes to somehow evaporate in our collective lifetimes.

They're here to stay.

While this long-term overview has been instructive, out-of-balance prices can be found in shorter time frames too—and they happen with great regularity. Finding profit opportunities that arise from these shorter-term extremes is at the heart of the 10-Minute Millionaire strategy.

Crazy Chickens

In May 2015—a mere three months after the company's IPO—shares of fast-casual restaurant Shake Shack Inc. (NYSE: SHAK) were already trading at stratospheric levels.

In fact, in the interest of specificity, let me quantify what I mean by "stratospheric."

The per-restaurant valuation reflected in Shake Shack's stock price was almost four times as high as the next closest competitor. In trading vernacular, the stock was on fire.

On May 20, 2015, a news service broke a story that a Shake Shack subsidiary had applied to trademark a chicken sandwich. Even though the trademark application had been filed a month earlier, traders and investors went full-on berserk. The company's stock—which was already trading at a price that was far above any rational, justifiable value—rocketed an additional 26 percent...in just three days.

All of this because a burger joint that wasn't even selling chicken sandwiches had registered a name—a full month before.

People (and by "people," I mean "investors") certainly get crazy.

The snapback move down from this price extreme was quick, decisive—and painful.

In the three trading days that came after Shake Shack shares achieved a new high, the company's stock skidded 26 percent. And just seven weeks later, the price had been cut in half.

Investors do get crazy.

The whole story is shown in one chart (see Figure 2.4).

Big profit opportunities don't manifest themselves when investors act rationally. They show up when people get crazy, get irrational and push prices to extremes.

Prices overrun to the upside—creating opportunities to "sell short" and cash in when the stocks revert back to more rational levels and plunge. (Pros sometimes refer to stocks in this situation as being "overbought.")

And prices also overrun to the downside—creating opportunities to go long and profit when the undervalued shares skyrocket to achieve a fair value. (Pros refer to stocks in this situation as being "oversold.")

Figure 2.4 Anatomy of an Extreme
SOURCE: Chart courtesy of StockCharts.com

Identifying these openings and framing trades that will let you capitalize can actually be a fairly simple proposition.

Indeed, when you focus on those extremes with the tools I've put together in this book, you'll find that investments of 10 minutes here, and 10 minutes there will be all you'll need to set up one big profit trade after another.

And if you just start by taking a small, underperforming piece of your portfolio, this strategy will be enough to help you turn that small pile of money into a big pile—and, ultimately, into a fortune.

Rubber-Band Man

The great thing about a strategy like this one is that there are countless ways to make money. Lots of money.

At the simplest level, here's what I mean.

When stocks, sectors, or entire indexes overrun to the upside, you can sell them short—and profit on the inevitable snapback decline. When those same investments are overrun to the downside, you can buy in and go long—cashing in on the eventual rebound.

While big market crashes are sensational and generate lots of media hype, I've learned that extremes are easier to play on the upside than on the downside. We can still identify profitable down-move opportunities, but the extremes that lead to down moves are more applicable to other trading strategies using advanced tools like put options and short positions. By focusing on long side trades and simple call options, we can generate bountiful returns without the lower probabilities and complexity that shorting can bring.

For our short-term price extremes, we'll be looking for pullbacks that have a high probability of snapping back to the upside. Here's a generic picture of what a pullback looks like:

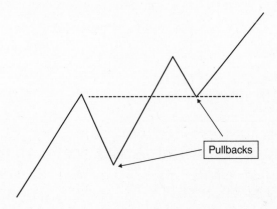

And Figure 2.5 is what that same sort of price action looks like on an actual stock chart. Figure 2.5 is a chart of one of the hot stocks (no pun intended) of late 2015 and early 2016 called First Solar Inc. (Nasdaq: FSLR).

As this chart illustrates, First Solar was moving up. But like most stocks in a long-term upward trend, it climbs the stairs in what traders refer to as "three-steps-up/one-step-back" pattern. *The 10-Minute Millionaire* is all about finding tradeable extremes like this so you can set up profitable trades.

As you'll see as we move forward, what I'm not talking about here is simple chart-reading. Divining stock moves from price charts alone is like predicting next week's weather based only on past temperatures.

It's a hit-or-miss proposition. Just as meteorologists include additional indicators like atmospheric pressure, wind speeds, and direction—and

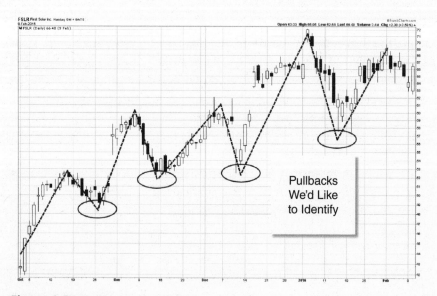

Figure 2.5   Pullbacks
SOURCE: Chart courtesy of StockCharts.com

cold and warm fronts—the toolset I'll be sharing will let you assemble a small-but-powerful data package that will let you reliably identify market extremes, ferret out false moves, and construct trades to profit from the snapback moves that follow.

Coming up, we'll show you how to identify and trade those short-term extremes. We'll give you one tool that warns of situations in which prices have moved too far too fast.

That tool will be fully explained in the chapters ahead, but for now I wanted to give you a sneak peek of how this indicator—called the "Relative Strength Indicator," or RSI—helps us identify those extremes. Just take a look at the Figure 2.6. The RSI is shown in the bottom portion.

This indicator helps us identify stocks that have reached short-term extremes. And it does this by calculating how far and how fast the stock price has moved. You can see that it helped us identify three of the four pullbacks in the FSLR chart. Indeed, only the first pullback did not trigger the signal because the pullback was too shallow. That means it didn't go very far, or very fast—telling us this may not be an actual extreme.

Now it's time to really get to work. Next, I'll walk you through the second fundamental concept of *The 10-Minute Millionaire:* it's time

Figure 2.6   "Sneak Peek"—Relative Strength Indicator (RSI)
SOURCE: Chart courtesy of StockCharts.com

to put the odds (probabilities) on your side in a way that gives you the chance to maximize your profits—while simultaneously minimizing potential losses.

In business, that's what's known as "getting an Edge."

And it works just as well in stocks as it does out in the marketplace.

We're going to show you how to "get an Edge" in the financial markets.

First, however, I want to share some specifics on market extremes.

There are several to watch for. They manifest themselves in distinct patterns. They each have unique characteristics.

Over time, you'll become quite adept at spotting them.

And when you perfected this talent, the profits will roll your way as you exploit them to maximum advantage.

BONUS CHAPTER 2A

The Millionaire's Cheat Sheet

The stock market is the story of cycles and of the human behavior that is responsible for overreactions in both directions.
      —Seth Klarman, noted value investor, author, and billionaire

Y ou may not recognize the name, but inside the hedge fund crowd Seth Klarman is viewed as one of investing's real legends. Klarman runs the Boston-based firm Baupost, which recently had $27 billion under management.

Klarman is known for achieving consistently high returns—despite often using unconventional strategies. A dyed-in-the-wool value investor who usually eschews the public spotlight, Klarman is nevertheless known for his ability to identify market extremes.

His favorite move is to identify extreme bargains—stocks, bonds, or other assets that are dramatically undervalued because they are way out of favor. In 2008, when many pundits were warning of a complete financial system collapse, Baupost was one of the few firms with the size, cash, and conviction to buy financial assets from distressed sellers (he even bought the badly thrashed bonds of collapsed Lehman Bros.)—positioning himself to cash in when the markets later rebounded.[2]

But with every investment he makes, Klarman also insists on a margin of safety—a value buffer that gives him some protection in case of unforeseen events.[3]

For a hedge fund billionaire like Klarman, a critical key to success is obviously preparation—meaningful research and due diligence on every potential investment. There's also, obviously, the benefit of years in the financial markets—a central part of which is being able to identify extremes when they occur.

Or, even better, to predict them before they happen.

For a retail investor, that need to find market extremes before they occur or even as they're playing out will probably seem like a daunting challenge.

And, for many investors, perhaps an insurmountable challenge.

But I'm going to let you in on a little secret...one that will short-circuit any fears you have—and ease your journey to 10-Minute Millionaire status.

And here's that secret.

There are really only three market extremes you have to worry about.

And each extreme has a unique "how often" and "how much" profile.

That means you'll know "how often" each extreme shows up in the financial markets. And it means you'll know "how much" you can expect to make from a trade properly executed against each extreme.

Consider this your Market Extreme Cheat Sheet.

And—like most cheat sheets (aka "crib sheets")—this one is so simple that you should be able to learn all of these patterns in...you guessed it...10 minutes or less.

Let's take a look together.

Market Extreme Number 1: The "Extreme Reversal" (rare to occur, but the most profitable of all when it does).

Market Extreme Number 1 actually comes in two flavors—and they are similar chart types with one key distinguishing characteristic. There's the Extremely Overbought flavor, in which the price of the stock or financial asset has gone straight up (up too far and too fast)—meaning it's poised for a pullback or snapback. And there's also the Extremely Oversold flavor, in which the stock or market has plunged, pushing the price level down well beyond what is reasonable—meaning it's poised for a spring back to the upside.

Let's look at both versions, using real examples to illustrate. And we'll start with the Overbought scenario (see Figure 2A.1).

Extremely Overbought scenarios have one characteristic that must be understood. Because investors have an optimistic bias (meaning prices have the same predisposition), individual stocks, sectors, and even entire markets can stay overbought for some time.

The extremes of this flavor that are the easiest to identify are those that hit parabolic territory, in which the price moves up like the shape of a parabola that we see in the Shake Shack chart shown in Figure 2A.1. As we'll see next, this is a bit different from what we see in the opposite scenario.

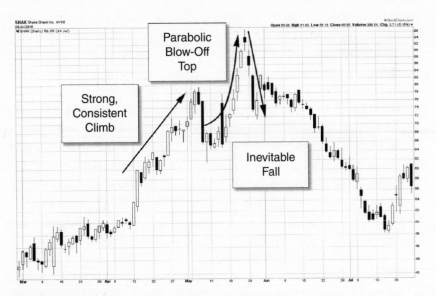

Figure 2A.1   Extreme Reversal Type 1—Overbought
SOURCE: Chart courtesy of StockCharts.com

Figure 2A.2   Extreme Reversal Type 2—Oversold
SOURCE: Chart courtesy of StockCharts.com

So let's turn to the second flavor, the Extremely Oversold situation. Here we're looking at something that's plummeted to an extreme, so much so that the price is poised for a snap back to the upside (see Figure 2A.2).

Again, thanks to the general bias to the upside, stocks, sectors, and indexes tend to bounce back sharply after a major drop.

In fact, 18 of the 20 largest single-day up moves in the Standard and Poor's 500 over the last 25 years were the result of Extremely Oversold snapbacks during massive bear moves.

Market Extreme Number 2: The Extreme Continuation (common to occur, which is great, since it, too, is very profitable).

Like the first extreme, Market Extreme Number 2 also comes in two flavors—and again are almost mirror images of each other. There's the Strong Stock scenario, in which a security has been *trending up*—but has then *pulled back* to a mid-term extreme on minor news (or no news at all). This positions the stock to rocket higher. There's also the Weak Stock scenario, in which a stock in a *downtrend* has been pushed *up* to a mid-term extreme on minor news (or no news at all). This positions the stock to drop like a stone.

Figure 2A.3   Extreme Continuation—Strong Stock
SOURCE: Chart courtesy of StockCharts.com

An example of the Strong Stock extreme is shown in Figure 2A.3.
And an example of a Weak Stock extreme is shown in Figure 2A.4.

Market Extreme Number 3: The Short-Term Extreme Turn-around—the most common of the extremes to occur, and the one that provides quick profits when it does. Because the turnarounds can be up or down, trading pros often refer to them as "Pops and Drops." (See Figure 2A.5.)

Pops and Drops occur when a stock is locked in a narrow (what pros call a "sideways") trading range—but the security is experiencing either a short-term extreme low or a short-term extreme high. If you can grab shares experiencing such extremes, you can profit when the share price snaps back and pops (from an extreme low) or drops (from an extreme high).

A point worth noting here is that the Rubber Band opportunities that we'll be talking about shortly are actually a type of pop—in the Pops and Drops.

When the Rubber Band (the price of a stock) gets stretched to the downside very quickly in a stock that has been, up to the time of the pullback, in a long-term uptrend, there is a high probability for a quick

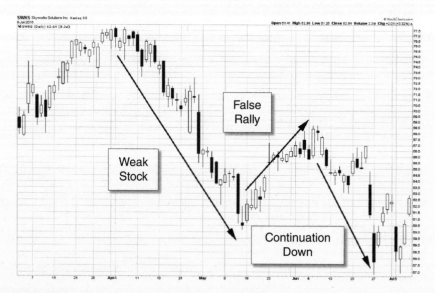

Figure 2A.4   Extreme Continuation—Weak Stock
SOURCE: Chart courtesy of StockCharts.com

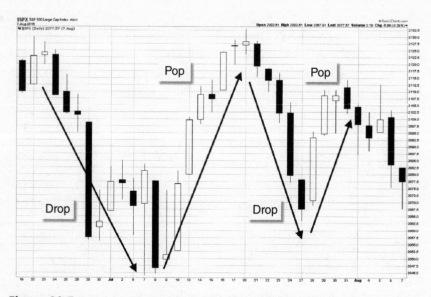

Figure 2A.5   Extreme Turnarounds—Pops and Drops
SOURCE: Chart courtesy of StockCharts.com

snapback to the upside. Drops are possible to play, too. But they pose more challenges and require extra steps in execution.

So, to keep things within our 10-Minute Millionaire framework, we'll focus on Pops (which happen often in up, down, and sideways markets) in the pages to come. And we'll leave the Drops to more seasoned traders.

Over a long stretch of trading, here's what you'll discover: short-term channel extreme pops and drops show up most often; mid-term continuation extremes in up and down directions happen moderately often; and extreme overbought and oversold reversals show up less frequently.

To visualize this frequency of occurrence of each of the price extremes I've been telling you about, take a look at this chart (Figure 2A.6).

What this chart actually does is to show the distribution frequency of the three Profit Pattern market price extremes that the 10-Minute Millionaire system is designed to help you profit from.

To review, then, as you trade you'll find that:

Short-Term Extreme Turnarounds (Pop and Drops):

- Occur most frequently.
- Give you quick action for quick profits.
- Happen in a short time frame.

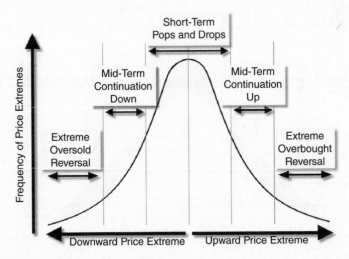

Figure 2A.6 Frequency of Stock Price Extremes

Extreme Continuations:

- Occur with moderate frequency.
- Offer moderate-to-large profit potential.
- Happen in an intermediate-term time frame.

And Extreme Reversals:

- Occur less frequently.
- Offer the biggest profit potential.
- Happen in a longer time frame.

Finding extremes is a key to helping us find the biggest profits. Fortunately for 10-Minute Millionaires, we can find tradeable extremes in all time frames.

That's an important point to underscore. Market extremes aren't just once-in-a-while opportunities that come along when the prices of individual stocks, business sectors, geographic economies, or entire asset classes get out of whack.

You'll find that a vigilant mindset—and an ability to recognize patterns like the ones we've shared with you here—will turn up other golden profit opportunities.

For example, intermediate-trend continuations can offer quick-strike profits when stock prices are seemingly going nowhere.

And like anything worth achieving in life, the more you practice, the more skilled you'll become.

And the more success you will have.

When you look back, you'll know that it all started here.

Notes

1. Ben. Y. Hayden, "Psychology, Not Economics, Is Behind Market Bubbles," *Psychology Today,* July 3, 2011.
2. Anonymous, "The Oracle of Boston," *The Economist,* July 7, 2012.
3. Ibid.

CHAPTER 3

How the "Potentate of Profits" Will Help You Get an Edge

Every strike brings me closer to the next home run.
—George Herman "Babe" Ruth

A s the afternoon sun dipped behind the west wall at Yankee Stadium in the Bronx during the next-to-last game of the 1927 baseball season, Babe Ruth stepped to the plate. For the 8,000 fans in attendance that Friday, the advancing shade offered a reprieve from the 86-degree beat-down. Out on the mound, hurler Tom Zachary was hoping to deliver a different kind of heat and finish off what had so far been an exceptionally well-pitched game against a team that could really swing the lumber.

Zachary's club—the Washington Senators—was tied 2–2 with the Bronx Bombers. It was the eighth inning...and two were out. The tall, stocky southpaw knew he'd had pretty good success against his lefty-swinging opponent, who so far had only two lifetime homers off his deliveries (as opposed to 10, 12, or more off other pitchers).

Even so, Zachary watched as the husky, 6-foot-2-inch slugger got set in the batter's box a mere 20 yards away. The pitcher knew the Babe was hungry for a win...as well as a very special place in the Major League Baseball record books.

Zach's first pitch was a fastball that split the plate for a strike. His second offering was high and tight—"a fast one at [Ruth's] big fat head," Zachary would later relate. It missed, but forced the Babe to hop awkwardly onto his back foot to keep from getting plunked.

The man known as "The Sultan of Swat" was used to "brushback" pitches, and rarely got mad. He preferred instead to get even. And in this case all he offered to Zachary was a bemused smirk.

A third pitch from the Senators' hurler ran the count to 2–1. The fourth pitch was low, inside...and fast.

Sensing a perfect setup, George Herman "Babe" Ruth strode into that pitch with his trademark swing. The crack of the bat was audible throughout the stadium. The Bambino gazed skyward...with nonchalance...as if watching a passing blimp drift by. The towering fly ball hugged the foul line and landed about halfway up the bleachers...fair by a mere 12 inches.

Zachary—a competitive pitcher who was known to kick dirt over the pitching rubber so he could move closer to the plate (as much as two feet closer, some said)—reportedly slammed his glove to the ground.

After a slow-but-deliberate jog around the bases, Babe Ruth's sixtieth homer of the season—13 more than runner-up Lou Gehrig, Ruth's teammate—was in the record books. It made the Babe the new all-time single-season home run king—setting a mark that would stand for 34 years.

Picking Your Spots

Babe Ruth will always be remembered as a slugger—hence such nicknames as the Great Bambino, the Caliph of Clout, the Big Bam, and the Behemoth of Bust (sportswriters used to compete with one another to see who could come up with the best new nickname for the Babe). Ruth was also known for high living. In 1925, his excesses led to "The bellyache heard 'round the world"—resulting in a seven-week hospital stay after surgery for what was described as an "intestinal abscess." (True to form, Ruth left the hospital, suited up on June 1—and hit 25 homers in the final 98 games of the season . . . a pace that would've equated to 40 in the full 154 games played at that time).

In his historic 1927 season—in addition to his record 60 homers— Ruth was also Number 1 in strikeouts, whiffing 89 times (stunning for the time but a far cry from the current single-season record of 223 set by Arizona Diamondback slugger Mark Reynolds back in 2009).

So let's take that deeper look at some of the Babe's other stats.

In 1927—in addition to leading the American League in homers and strikeouts—The Sultan of Swat also ranked first for bases on balls (137), runs scored (158), and on-base percentage (.486). Despite all of these amazing league-topping stats, the Babe only ranked a distant ninth in batting (despite hitting a scorching .356) and failed to crack the Top 10 in base hits (192).

Here are four specific conclusions we can reach—and lessons we can learn—from those statistics.

And each of these four applies directly to investing . . .

First, Ruth was a careful and particular hitter—and waited for "his" pitch . . . for something he could really *drive.*

Second, he wasn't afraid to let an "imperfect" pitch pass by—even if he knew it would be called a strike. He viewed each pitch as an "opportunity"—and was willing to eschew less-than-perfect setups.

Third, he didn't swing at "junk"—pitches outside the strike zone— as evidenced by his league-leading walks total.

Finally, Ruth accepted that occasional strikeouts were part of the game . . . and knew that if he went down on strikes in one at bat, he'd get other chances later in the same game, or in the next one. Strikeouts, he believed, were permissible—part of an opportunity mix that gave him other opportunities to score.

The bottom line: in contrast to his image as a free-swinging, high-living slugger, Babe Ruth was actually a patient, selective hitter, who took what pitchers gave him . . . *and made the most of each individual opportunity.* He got on base more frequently than anyone else in the league. And he scored more runs than anyone else in the league. He hit a lot of homers...but he also accepted singles and walks—knowing that even those gave him the chance to score.

In short, during his playing days, Babe Ruth was a living, breathing practitioner of the wisdom...the values...and the mindset...that underpins the 10-Minute Millionaire trading system.

So like the sportswriters of those halcyon years, we are also going to take our shot at creating a new moniker for the Babe.

Just call him the "Potentate of Profits."

In the decades since Ruth's record-setting performance, investment sages and trading gurus have focused on this low-strikeout/high-homer ratio as a goal to aspire to.

And tucked within that goal is a lesson...a powerful lesson, in fact. And here's its essence.

Take *enough* swings, and you're bound to hit some homers.

And if you take the *right* swings—meaning you take what the pitcher (the market) is giving you, and don't try to do more than is possible (you don't swing for 10-bagger stocks and you don't risk every penny you've got on every single trade)—you'll amass an enviable record.

Indeed, you'll amass a *very* enviable record.

You *will* strike out—that's unavoidable. But those whiffs will be *more than offset* by the walks, singles, doubles, and triples you amass.

And the homers.

Take this approach—as a hitter *or* as an investor—and you'll score early and often. You won't amass too many strikeouts.

We refer to this philosophy as "giving yourself an Edge."

Ruth understood this—and became a Hall of Fame slugger. The Colonial Minutemen knew this—and engineered a historic turning point in a war that appeared lost.

Do this as an investor—and you'll amass *a fortune*.

To do this, you need to know how to get an Edge—*your* Edge.

And I'm going to show you how to do so by breaking your search for an Edge down into its three component parts:

1. Maximize your *expected return*. Most traders think about their upside potential on a trade-by-trade basis. But most traders are completely wrong. The 10-Minute Millionaire views upside potential as statistical

probabilities over a large number of trades. This probabilistic approach keeps us focused like a laser on the productive process of building true wealth. And it also neutralizes our natural biases and irrational self-destructive behavior.

2. Minimize your *downside risk*. Rookies believe that big wins and home runs are the key to successful trading. The 10-Minute Millionaire knows that the first and foremost objective is actually limiting losses. What Wall Street pros refer to as "downside risk" isn't just a *component* of gaining a probabilistic Edge in the market. The fact is that downside risk *defines* that Edge.

3. Determine your optimal *position sizing*. Even with a huge market Edge, a 10-Minute Millionaire investor knows that probability is a key element of your long-term success. To build meaningful wealth in the investing markets, we need to do *lots* of trades, each with a high probability of success. Sizing each position correctly is mission-critical if you're to stay alive long enough to reap big gains even when the market temporarily turns against you. I'll show you the right way to make this happen each and every time. Embrace the strategy and you'll avoid the biggest risk of all—blowing up your account.

Great Expectations

What is an "Edge" (or a "positive expectancy," if we're feeling fancy)? Put simply:

$$Edge = Expected\ Return - Downside\ Risk$$

If it looks like a simple equation, that's because . . . well . . . it is. But there's elegance in that simplicity.

That equation's simplicity obscures the fact that it's actually a very powerful tool. And when you use that tool correctly and diligently, it will lead you to unparalleled wealth.

In truth, this equation is a gift. So let's take a minute to unpack it and examine the individual, underlying elements.

The idea of "expected return" is pretty easy to grasp, at least mathematically. And if you break it into the individual pieces that I mentioned a minute ago, it gets even simpler. There are two of those pieces, and they are:

1. A short-term *variance around* an expected return
2. And a long-term *convergence to* an expected return

Years ago, back in engineering school, I had a really great physics teacher who had a gift for taking really tough concepts and making them seem simple. It was his approach that made him so talented. For instance, whenever he was introducing a new topic, he would always start by telling us about an "ideal" scenario. He'd isolate certain variables—like friction or mass—so we could more clearly focus on such underlying concepts as momentum. Once we learned how the math worked in the conceptually simplified world of frictionless planes and massless pulleys, he'd introduce real-world complexities—but always one new variable at a time.

We'll use the same approach here to dissect expected return with an easy-to-understand example of a zero sum game. This way you can more easily understand the concepts of variance and convergence before we move on to more complex concepts involving positive returns and downside risk.

To see what I mean, consider the following thought experiment.

Let's say we take 100 chits—numbered sequentially from a negative $50 to a positive $50—and place them in a bag.

If I randomly draw one chit—and either pay the face value (for a negative number) or reap that value (with a positive-numbered chit)—after that single draw I could find that I'm $50 richer, $50 poorer, or anything in between. That's a pretty big variance. But if I keep drawing, accumulating the gains and losses, and then discarding each chit, by the time I get to the hundredth chit, I'll be at a perfect breakeven.

It's guaranteed. We've set up the bag to be exactly balanced in value so that all the negative chits will exactly cancel out the positive ones. It couldn't happen any other way. For this particular (simplified) experiment, we say that my expected return is zero—hence the term zero sum game.

Now let's add a thin layer of complexity and change this "guaranteed" zero sum exercise to one that's "probabilistically" zero sum.

To do this, we'll add the element of "replacement"—meaning instead of keeping each chit after every draw, I'll put it back in the bag so it could potentially be drawn again.

Now the game outcome isn't perfectly determined. With each chit eligible to be redrawn, I could conceivably draw, for example, $50 five times in a row. At the end of 100 draws, it's anyone's guess what my final balance will be, right?

Not really. A funny thing happens when we run a probabilistic system over many, many trials. Even if I replace each chit back in the bag after each turn, I may not come out at precisely breakeven by the hundredth draw, but the laws of statistics say I'll be pretty darn close. To see this visually, take a look at the example of five simulated runs of the 50/50 chit exercise I described. Mentally picture this as five friends... each drawing from five separate bags over the course of 100 draws. (See Figure 3.1.)

On the first pick, Alex was up $45 (Yahoo!). Brian lost $40. Cheryl was down $22. David lost $11. And with a negative $2, Ellen was essentially at breakeven. That's a pretty wide disparity in returns. Indeed, if each player had started the game with a mere $10 in their pockets, all but two would be wiped out on the first round of the game.

Ouch ...

But look what happens after just 10 draws. The average returns begin to converge. Now the swing isn't a negative $40 to a positive $45, it's a negative $13 to a positive $8.

And see what happens after the full 100 trials (Figure 3.2). All five friends are hovering right around our expected value of breakeven and nobody goes home with a gain or loss greater than a buck or so.

From here, you can clearly see the two major components of a probabilistic system like the one I'll teach you in the pages ahead. Namely, in the short term, returns can and will vary widely across large ranges of gains and losses. But more importantly, over the long run, those returns converge through the laws of probability to a known expected return—even if (or maybe more accurately, *especially* if) the process is purely random.

Of course I'd never actually put on a trade with a zero (or negative) expectancy. But that's *precisely* what the typical trader does when he or she buys into an overbought (overpriced) stock... or when they step up to the roulette wheel in Las Vegas.

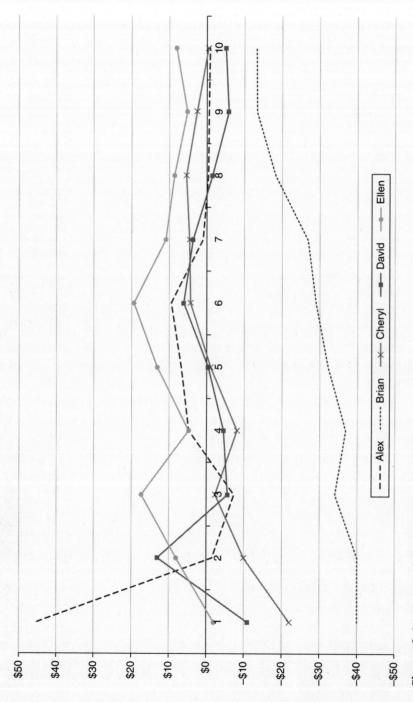

Figure 3.1 Expected Return: Short-Term Variance

62

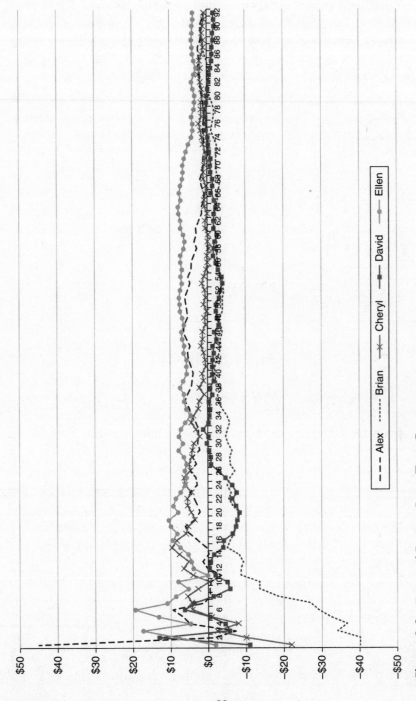

Figure 3.2 Expected Return: Long-Term Convergence

The 10-Minute Millionaire trading system fixes the left side of our Edge equation—our expected return—by successfully identifying extreme market conditions. When market conditions are favorable, the 10-Minute Millionaire is right about two-thirds of the time, with average gains of 9 percent to 10 percent or more for stock trades and as much as 15 percent to 20 percent for more highly leveraged options plays. The result is an expected return on each stock trade of around 6 percent to 7 percent (if we display that mathematically, it looks like: $0.66 \times 0.10 = 6.66$ percent).

As they say, it's always better to show than to tell, so let's put some meat on the bone so you can see how impactful this could be.

Theoretically, by doing just one trade per week for a 7 percent gain, an initial $2,500 investment would double itself four times to almost $79,000 in a year.

This sounds pretty good, right?

But we're missing out on one huge part of the Edge equation: What's the downside if I'm wrong?

Risky Business

When I discuss trading with folks who are new to the game, they almost always want to talk about how big the winners can be or how often a strategy is right. By contrast, every time I've sat down with a professional trader to talk shop, assess strategies, or model systems, the *first thing* they always talk about is risk management. And I literally mean *every* time.

Most investors believe that gains—profits—are the key part of the trading equation. But as a professional who's served as a risk-management officer for a hedge fund for more than a decade, I know that risk is the key. I could have all the expected upside return in the world, but if my risk exceeds it, I'm sunk.

To see this in action, take another simple example.

Let's say I enter a rigged coin-flipping contest in which the payout is always $1.00 for a correct guess (and $0.00 for an incorrect guess). With a 50/50 chance of being right, my expected return is 50 cents. The law of averages says that after 100 rounds, I'd pocket about $50 and head over to a nice restaurant for a steak dinner (a real steak dinner . . . not one of the early bird specials). All you have to do is play and you get an assured payout.

This is how most amateur traders view the market. They focus only on the potential upside. By taking that approach, though, they are ignoring the *single most important element* in the quest to gain an Edge—namely, the money I have to put at risk...just to play the game.

For example, if it costs me 50 cents to flip the coin, I have a net-expected return of zero—just like in our random chit example. In this case, we'd say there is no Edge; the game is exactly even—(that is, 50 cents of expected return minus 50 cents of capital at risk).

This sounds like a pretty stupid bet. But at least it's not terribly destructive. I may win a few tosses... or lose a few. Over time, I should come out about where I started.

If on the other hand, the cost of entry was 75 cents, I'd be playing a game of *certain* financial destruction.

While my expected gain is still 50 cents, the cost of entry guarantees that I'll lose, on average, a quarter (25 cents) on each and every flip of the coin... (See Figure 3.3.)

While this sounds idiotic, it's exactly what most traders do in the market—every single day.

Traders employ a vocabulary all their own. And when they take a position—on a stock, broad market, or on an options or futures contract—which, by definition, means they're taking a risk—they talk about putting on a trade.

Most of the time, they put on perfectly good trades (trades with excellent upside potential).

But they end up losing money—by not managing their downside risk.

In short, they approach their trades from the wrong point of view... by emphasizing the wrong thing.

		Game 1	Game 2	Game 3
Identical Returns on 50/50 Coin Flip ⟹	Expected Return	$0.50	$0.50	$0.50
Money at Risk = Cost to Play ⟹	Downside Risk	$0.75	$0.50	$0.25
Profit Driven by Risk, Not Return ⟹	Edge	–$0.25	$0.00	**$0.25**

Figure 3.3 Controlling Risk Drives Positive Returns

In contrast, what the 10-Minute Millionaire does is identify trades with high expected returns—those stocks that have been pulled to extremes by irrational markets... and that are ready for a big snapback.

And 10-Minute Millionaire investors then get a huge Edge by limiting their downside risk.

To see this in action, consider the following example. Let's say I've identified an extreme trading opportunity on a $60 stock that has a two-thirds chance of snapping back for a $9 gain. The typical greenhorn trader will think that sounds like pretty good odds, so they jump right in with exactly zero downside protection, even though the stock could fall 50 percent or even more.

Here's how it looks mathematically:

Edge = Expected return − Downside risk

Expected return = 2/3 (Chance of a gain)

×$9 (Potential gain on trade) = $6

Downside risk = 1/3 (Chance of a loss)

×$30 (Potential loss on trade) = $10

$6 − $10 = (minus $4)

In other words, if the greenhorn puts on enough of these negative expectancy trades, they'll lose four bucks per trade, on average. Not each and every time, mind you. Two out of three individual trades will be winners, but over time the size of the less-frequent losses will pretty much ensure total financial destruction.

The reality is that very few stocks are going to completely crash and burn for a total loss—but they could. And even if the realistic downside isn't as extreme as a 30-point loss, without a defined exit strategy we're still leaving any chance at positive Edge—and our very trading survival—totally to chance.

Now take a look at what happens when we do that exact same trade the 10-Minute Millionaire way.

We'll take that predetermined expected return and turn those money-losing odds dramatically in our favor simply by controlling the downside risk.

Expected return = 2/3 (Chance of a gain)

$\qquad$ ×$9 (Potential gain on trade) = $6

Downside risk = 1/3 (Chance of a loss)

$\qquad$ ×$6 (Potential loss on trade) = $2

$\qquad$ $6 − $2 = $4

Now, instead of losing $4 on every turn of the crank on my trading system, I'm making $4 of profit. Sure, I'll lose six bucks one out of three times on average, but the two $9 wins will more than make up for the losses.

Sounds like a winning plan, but how exactly do you limit your downside? One way is just by setting a mental limit for your trade. "I'll just sell if the price drops to $54," says the slightly evolved newbie.

It's a thoughtful step in the right direction . . . but it's still an approach that's riddled with problems.

First and foremost, markets move quickly and unexpectedly. Setting a mental limit (a "mental stop" in that trader's parlance) means I'll be *tied* to my stock ticker, and forced to monitor the market's every move during trading hours.

That's an investment of time way beyond the 10 minutes a day of my system.

Second, even if I do flag the stock at my mental limit, what's to ensure I don't second-guess myself and decide to hold on for a possible turnaround rather than take a certain loss?

The 10-Minute Millionaire system shows us a better way.

A much better way . . .

A Blueprint for Winning

You may not recognize the name Denis Waitley. But I'll bet you recognize his better-known works. Waitley, an American motivational speaker, consultant, and author is known for his audio series *The Psychology of Winning* and such books as *The Winner's Edge*.

I mention him here because of one particular comment he made that's always resonated with me.

According to Waitley, "Losers make promises they often break. Winners make commitments they always keep."

Successful traders—the most-seasoned pros—live by this mindset. Newbies don't.

It's all about *creating a plan* for managing risk—and *maintaining* that commitment.

Let me show you what I mean . . .

The first concern for pro traders is: "Where do I get out if I'm wrong?"

In other words, the pros don't start each trading day asking themselves: "How big a profit can I bag today?"

They already *know* how much they can make with their system—on average, over time, as is the case with our 10-Minute Millionaire trading system.

Their *real aim* is to stay at the plate . . . so they can keep swinging at trades—hitting singles, getting walks, and slugging the occasional homer . . . and scoring lots of runs . . . while keeping the strikeouts to acceptable levels.

These pros, you see, are Babe Ruth traders . . . they're 10-Minute Millionaires in the making.

The 10-Minute Millionaire takes a two-pronged approach to managing risk, because it puts a big emphasis on:

1. Contingency exits (more commonly known as "stop-losses") for each trade.
2. And position sizing, a device that helps control risk through the careful management of the number of shares or contracts that you trade.

These two elements of the risk-management part of your trading strategy work in tandem: They *minimize* your risk component and *maximize* your trading Edge.

Getting into a trade is a pretty simple task, both mechanically (the click of a mouse) and psychologically (each trade is full of potential and hope).

It's just the exit that's tough.

All investors want to make money and avoid losses. They want to avoid being wrong.

So it's kind of surprising how few of these folks mentally walk all the way through a trade—looking at every contingency . . . and even rehearsing their exit strategy—before actually pulling the trigger to put on the trade.

I refer to this as "seeing my way out of a trade."

And I do it with every investment or trade I'm considering.

Every trade needs a predetermined way out...you know, an exit plan for every conceivable contingency. In the daily auction we know as the stock market, we never know when the herd mentality will turn against even the best-researched and best-located trade entry.

That's where the all-important exit-strategy tool called the "stop-loss" comes into the picture.

A stop-loss is a standing order to sell your stock (or option) if it trades at or below a predetermined price. (See Figure 3.4.)

For example, let's say you buy 100 shares of XYZ Corp. at $20 each. At the same time, you enter a sell-stop order at $18. As long as the stock price stays above $18, your position is safe. If, however, the market tanks and XYZ hits your stop price, the position will immediately sell

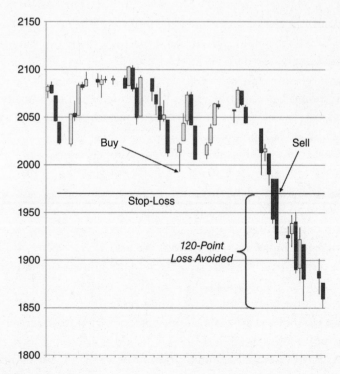

Figure 3.4 Stop-Loss

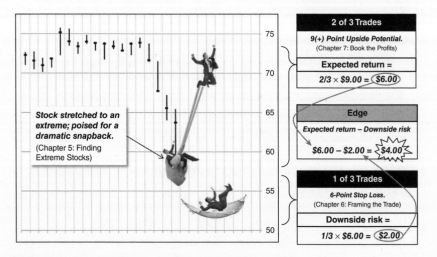

Figure 3.5   The 10-Minute Millionaire's Trading Edge
NOTE: Illustration Only. Actual parameters for each trading opportunity are individual and unique and determined by the 10-Minute Millionaire system.

at the market. Stops are an extremely simple and powerful way to excise emotion from the trading process and maintain your positive Edge by limiting losses to a predefined level.

Figure 3.5 shows how it looks in the context of our Edge example.

This should be foolproof, right? We can predetermine our downside risk while preserving all of our upside? It sounds like the definition of "ultimate Edge." What could go wrong?

At some point—and this is an absolute certainty—you *will* get stopped out at the bottom of a reversal. (See Figure 3.6.) That's a reality you have to expect... and accept.

The stock will hit your stop, you'll be out of your position, and then the price will do a "180 reversal" and rebound to new highs. It happens. And it happens more often than we'd like.

After seeing this a time or two—and being human—your mind will begin to concoct wild conspiracy theories.

Maybe some floor trader saw your stop on the books and deliberately sold a big block to take you out before buying up a bargain.

You will feel burned and betrayed. And you'll start asking yourself: Should the stops be set at a different price... or maybe not used at all?

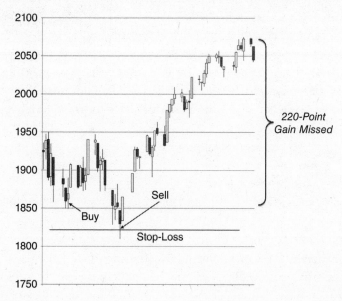

Figure 3.6   Stop-Out

After all, the stop order that was supposed to protect your downside ended up costing you a huge upside gain on a great trade. The next time around, you'll be tempted to adjust your stops—move them down—if the stock price starts edging close to that trigger point.

Don't make that mistake.

Because it's a big one.

It's the avoidance of such basic but costly errors as this that will separate successful 10-Minute Millionaire investors like you from the typical market trading plebe.

In fact, the tendency for new traders to move or cancel stops as the price gets close to them is so prevalent that it even has a name.

Old pros call it a "cancel if close" order... a reference to a risk-management stop that won't be kept.

Over time, you'll get past this urge. You'll mind-meld with the Babe, accepting the occasional whiff because of all the walks, singles, and doubles you're getting... and all the runs you're scoring—punctuated with enough homers to add zeros to your net worth.

Just keep remembering: you don't have to be right all the time to make a ton of money in the markets.

It's okay to be wrong here and there—even fairly frequently—as long as you have these two things working for you:

1. A system that pays off much more than it costs you, over time.
2. And a risk-management system that avoids bet-the-ranch investments and that keeps the losses you inevitably have to low-enough levels.

Do that and you *will* make money.
Lots of money.
In fact, you'll make a fortune.
To do that, however, you must become *excellent* at defending your capital.

Indeed, in my talks with new investors and in my sessions with the high-net-worth investors I've worked with over time, here's the message I drive home over and over and over again: "Until you can consistently keep your stop discipline—always setting stops and always exiting positions when those stops are hit—no other aspect of trading really matters."

It's that fundamental. And it's that important.

The reality is that more trading accounts are crushed for lack of stops—or lack of a stop discipline—than any other reason that I've seen. Here again, our Number 1 human foible—making decisions based on emotion instead logic—is our single-biggest/single-worst enemy. Just setting up a stop isn't enough. It takes discipline to keep it in place and to keep from succumbing to our emotions and irrational psychology that prods us to move it lower . . . or cancel it altogether.

Stop the Loss/Stop the Pain

The characterization of trades as "winners" or as "losers" is another big reason that new traders do stupid things and move their stops. We naturally avoid what is bad and keep what is good. If a trade that hits its contingency exit is bad in your mind, there will be a desire to keep that bad thing from happening.

So as the price of your investment approaches that stop point, the temptation to move the stop order down (or cancel it completely) could become too great, leading to even bigger losses.

On the other hand, if a profitable trade is defined as good, we want to make sure that we collect that trading goodness. This can lead to taking profits too quickly, so we actually get to pocket the gains.

Wanting to keep good trades good also leads to trader skittishness with profitable trades. When a trade is modestly profitable and then takes a short-term dip, a natural reaction is to exit the trade too quickly to preserve what is now a small profit. That's understandable; you want to be able to feel good about the trade.

Clearly, classifying winning trades as "good" and losing trades as "bad" can engender all sorts of problematic behavior.

This undesirable activity is the exact opposite of the 10-Minute Millionaire approach that says we should cut our losses short and let our winners run.

Getting to that approach means you have to embrace a new way of thinking about your trades, about your winners and losers. Reclassify them in your mind as profitable and unprofitable or expected and unexpected.

Here's the ultimate key to success: the *best* traders totally dispense with those value-based perceptions (being good or bad), and learn to accept occasional money-losing trades as just part of the game.

Great traders are absolute masters at the mental part of framing a trade. They can see their way out of a trade that's a loser and hits its contingency stop. And they accept it with no second-guessing or personal recriminations.

Those losers are just the cost of doing business. They are neither good nor bad—they just are part of the system.

If you find yourself struggling to be a winner by keeping your commitments—maintaining your stops when your trade moves against you—you've got plenty of company.

But don't despair.

In fact, let me share the four tricks I teach my students to help them honor their stops—that is, keeping their risk-management commitments. They are:

1. Write It Down: Here I'm saying you should literally take pen to paper and write out your stop price. This sounds like a pretty simple trick—and it is. But research shows that if we write something

down, we're much more likely to keep the commitment than if we just make a mental note. There's something about the physical act of writing, the visual nature of seeing the number, and even the auditory reminder of saying it out loud as your write it that makes it a real commitment.

The best way to make this a routine commitment is to start and keep a trading log. Just grab a notebook and create a few simple column headings: date, symbol, entry price, stop-price, and profit target. Or use the trading worksheet provided at the end of this book and at www.10-minutemillionaire.com.

This is *such* a big deal, I'm even going to ask you to go a step further and demonstrate your personal commitment to keep your stop. Sign your initials for each trade entry. Now you're adding extra incentive—to keep the "contract" you just made with yourself. I've been trading for years, and I still do this with my own trades.

2. Reward the "Right Moves": For some folks, unfortunately, even writing their stop price on paper is not enough to overcome a nonexistent stop discipline. If you find that you're still having trouble setting and keeping your stops, implement a "reward" system. When I was starting to trade on an active basis, I found that my emotions would occasionally swamp my strategy—meaning I was sometimes moving a stop or ignoring it altogether.

Naturally, I couldn't let this continue. So to keep this from becoming a damaging bad habit, I took a drastic step.

It involved chocolate.

I put a jar on my desk right beside my trading computer and filled it with Peanut M&Ms. Every time I executed a stop correctly, I allowed myself to enjoy the chocolatey, peanutty goodness of a single M&M. If I didn't keep my stop discipline—no treat. Before long I was keeping my stop every time I made one.

3. Don't Waver: Once you have set your stop-loss, never move it further away from your entry point. And I mean *not for any reason*. This ironclad discipline will let you dodge a whole lot of heartache over your trading career.

Think of your commitment to your stop-loss strategy as a fundamental core value. A set-in-stone belief. In trading—as in life—temptations come along all the time. But we fight those temptations.

We don't want to betray our core values. Indeed, we want to display courage, an admirable core quality. It takes courage to ignore emotion during tough markets. But that's want we want to do with our stops. Don't be a sellout.

4. **Be True to Yourself:** Everyone's "pain point"—the slang term for "risk tolerance"—is different. But every investor needs to know his or her pain point. You need to understand just how much risk...how much of a loss...is acceptable. Your financial goals, your emotional makeup, and even your age all will be factors. Once you understand this, you can determine how many shares or contracts you can trade based on your total dollars risked per trade and how far your stop is from your entry point. This adjusts your total risk per trade to a level that is right for you. In the next section, we'll take an in-depth look at how to calculate the number of shares or contracts per trade.

Another Step toward Success

Now that we're prepared to have a defined contingency exit for each trade, developed the discipline to honor our stops, and have captured a gigantic trading Edge in the market, we should be all set—right?

Not quite.

Now, it's true that getting an Edge in the market is fundamental to trading success, but we still run the risk of blowing ourselves up by risking too much of our capital on a single trade or two.

It's important to remember the fundamental properties of probabilistic systems:

- Returns will converge in the long term.
- But they can vary wildly in the short term.

So even though I'm controlling my downside risk on any given trade, a series of short-term stop-losses can wipe me out if I risk too much each time.

To see what I mean, let's look at a series of 12 trades—each with a two-thirds chance of a 75-point gain and a one-third chance of a 50-point loss.

Theoretically, my expected return over many trials is $33.33 per trade (2/3 × 75 − 1/3 × 50). Over 12 trades, I should be up 400 points on average (12 trades × $33.33 = $400 *expected return*).

Now, let's say the trades worked out as follows:

Total Capital	$100.00											
At Risk	$50.00											
Trade #	1	2	3	4	5	6	7	8	9	10	11	12
Outcome	Loss	Loss	Win	Loss	Win	Win	Win	Loss	Win	Win	Win	Win
Gain	0.00	0.00	75.00	0.00	75.00	75.00	75.00	0.00	75.00	75.00	75.00	75.00
Loss	50.00	50.00	0.00	50.00	0.00	0.00	0.00	50.00	0.00	0.00	0.00	0.00
Profit (Loss)	(50.00)	(50.00)	75.00	(50.00)	75.00	75.00	75.00	(50.00)	75.00	75.00	75.00	75.00
Total Return	(50.00)	(100.00)	(25.00)	(75.00)	0.00	75.00	150.00	100.00	175.00	250.00	325.00	400.00
Capital Reserve	$50.00	$0.00	$0.00	$0.00	$0.00	$0.00	$0.00	$0.00	$0.00	$0.00	$0.00	$0.00

Overall, my expected return worked out—just as I expected. Eight out of 12 (or two-thirds) of my trades were winners, so my total return after 12 runs was 400 points. Exactly as predicted.

This looks great until I remember that I had only $100 of capital in reserve and I risked 50 percent of it on each of the first two trades. After two drawdowns of $50 each, I'm completely wiped out and can't capitalize on the wins that follow.

That's not savvy investing . . .

Instead, let's say I rewind the clock and take a second crack at the exact same trade with identical Edge and matching outcomes. This time, however, I'll manage my position size. I'll risk only 10 percent of my capital on any one trade—or $10 of my $100 capital reserve.

Here's how it looks on this go-round:

Total Capital	$100.00											
At Risk	$10.00											
Trade #	1	2	3	4	5	6	7	8	9	10	11	12
Outcome	Loss	Loss	Win	Loss	Win	Win	Win	Loss	Win	Win	Win	Win
Gain	0.00	0.00	15.00	0.00	15.00	15.00	15.00	0.00	15.00	15.00	15.00	15.00
Loss	10.00	10.00	0.00	10.00	0.00	0.00	0.00	10.00	0.00	0.00	0.00	0.00
Profit (Loss)	(10.00)	(10.00)	15.00	(10.00)	15.00	15.00	15.00	(10.00)	15.00	15.00	15.00	15.00
Total Return	(10.00)	(20.00)	(5.00)	(15.00)	0.00	15.00	30.00	20.00	35.00	50.00	65.00	80.00
Capital Reserve	$90.00	$80.00	$95.00	$85.00	$100.00	$115.00	$130.00	$120.00	$135.00	$150.00	$165.00	$180.00

Now the string of trades looks like gold.

With the exact same expected return, I came out a winner through proper position sizing.

By reserving enough capital to weather the downturns inherent in any probabilistic system, I managed to stay flush long enough to realize some big gains. In fact, I didn't even start to turn an overall profit until Trade Number 5—and that's okay. From then on, I was in the black despite losing along the way again on Trade Number 8.

Previously, I blew up my entire capital base of $100 before I even got started. This time, I walked away with an $80 profit.

And to stress this point—because it's so very important—these winning results are on the *exact* same string of trades. The *only* difference was the size of my position.

By ratcheting down my risk exposure, I gave up a $400 expected return for a mere $80 in profits.

While that qualifies as a "tradeoff," here's how a 10-Minute Millionaire would view these two sets of outcomes.

If you think about it carefully, what I *really* gave up here wasn't the added gain. It was the huge and very real risk of financial destruction. In return for that tradeoff, I received a near-certain chance for a smaller-but-solid gain. I'd rather have 20 percent of something than 100 percent of nothing every day of the week.

So this capstone of our risk-management toolkit is something called "position sizing." This is the part of your trading strategy that answers two crucial questions:

1. How much am I willing to risk per trade?
2. And how many shares or contracts should I trade as a result?

Sizing Up Your Opportunity

When I think back to my work as a chemical engineer in charge of starting up two very dangerous and very different chemical plants—one a uranium processor and the other a methane/propane cracking facility—I understand why I'm such a stickler for sound risk management.

Indeed, my focus on safety and obsession with risk minimization has been such a central component of my thinking for so long that it's now second nature.

And with good reason.

For example, a misstep at the uranium facility would have exposed thousands of people to radiation. The second startup—cracking methane and propane at very high temperatures—was actually even more dangerous. The smallest leak of oxygen into the containment system could have turned an entire city block into a deep, dark (and probably still-smoking) hole in the ground.

Obviously, none of that happened (it would otherwise have been international news). Because I was obsessive about risk.

And I brought that fanatical focus on risk management with me into the financial markets. I was drawn to the field of risk management and position sizing early on. As I got my start in the markets almost three decades ago, a basic knowledge of these principles saved my bacon more than once... especially in the early going.

Just how crucial is position sizing to the overall management of risk? The most notorious trading blowups in history—from Jérôme Kerviel at Société Générale and Nicholas Leeson at Barings Bank to Brian Hunter at Amaranth Advisors and the whole gang at Long-Term Capital Management—all share one single trait.

Without exception, each had *way too much capital* devoted to a *single* idea.

The takeaway: when it comes to trading, position sizing is the single-biggest reason that accounts get blown up.

To make this point in the private investing seminars I've taught, I run my students through a couple of scenarios.

I start by having those students "tightrope walk" the length of a single piece of 2 × 4 lumber—while that board is sitting flat on the ground.

Most folks make that journey—traverse the board—from one end to the other with no trouble at all. And if they happen to fall... well, so what? We're talking about a modest plunge of... two inches. (Okay, it's actually 1½ inches; as most of the do-it-yourselfers out there know, one of the sordid secrets of the building business is that those 2 × 4 boards just aren't as thick as advertised.)

Once these folks have made a few practice runs, they're skipping, running, even moonwalking from one end of the board to the other. They're completely comfortable and know that even if they stumble, it's no big deal.

Next, however, I tell those same students to imagine that the same 2 × 4 is stretched between the roofs of two tall—but not quite side by side—buildings. I ask if they'd like to do the same simple exercise of walking across the board in this new, eminently more risky configuration.

Each person's ability to walk across the board is exactly the same as when it was down at ground level. The degree of difficulty hasn't changed. But the consequences have shifted—dramatically. The cost of a misstep has changed from being mildly embarrassing to tragically fatal.

The same is true when you identify a trade that has a high probability of being profitable (meaning it has a positive Edge). Now if you put too much money in that single stock, that probability doesn't change . . . but the consequences you face if that trade goes wrong are now potentially fatal to your finances.

At that point in my classes—thanks to that comparison—every single student has the same visceral reaction . . . and immediately understands the risk of betting too much money on a single trade.

When you're just getting started as a trader, your position-sizing calculation is a simple one. Just trade the smallest units possible. Literally one share of stock per trade or one option contract. The last thing you want is to plunk down a large amount of money when you're moving into a new system or strategy. You don't want to wipe out your stake as you learn to trade.

If trading a single share of stock seems boring, consider this. I have taught full three-day seminars exclusively on position-sizing algorithms and taught shorter sections on risk management . . . to literally *thousands* of people. I've brought this same message to several hundred thousand more folks in my earlier best-selling book, in guest columns I've penned, and in the newsletters I run.

So I've told lots of traders to start small. And not one person has ever come back to me and said, *"You know, D.R., your advice to trade small at the beginning has ruined my life."*

In fact, quite the opposite has happened. Plenty of folks have told me that trading small has saved them from untold losses while they were test flying a new strategy.

And don't fret about the cost associated with "trading small." Thanks to deregulation, online brokers, and the emergence of self-directed electronic trading, the once high cost of trading small blocks or odd lots has disappeared.

Besides, how do you really define "expensive?" Is it burning a few extra dollars on commissions as a form of tuition to learn a new wealth-creating system? Or is it losing *thousands* on a trade gone wrong before you learn the ropes—perhaps even a big-enough loss to chase you to the sidelines, so that you never trade again?

A final thought on this point: some brokerages now offer commission-free trading for a period of time as an incentive to open a new account, which takes the commission excuse completely off the table.

When do you start trading larger blocks? After you've achieved a rate of breakeven or better for a few months or more, then you can start to ramp up your position size.

Once you're ready to step up, let's take a look at the right and the wrong way to establish position sizes for the greatest possible trading Edge.

It's Better to Weight for an Edge
Than to Wait for an Edge

Splitting your money into equal parts has always been an easy way to allocate money across trades. If you have $100,000—and want to invest it in five equal parts—you would buy $20,000 worth of each of the five stocks you're looking at. So if you're taking a position in a $100 stock, you would buy 200 shares; for a $50 stock, you buy 400 shares, and so on. We'll call this *equal-dollar weighting*.

A more sophisticated approach is to use your stop-loss level for each position to determine the per-share risk that you are taking for a given trade. Once you know your risk amount for each trade, you can calculate how many shares to buy based on how much of your total portfolio you would be willing to risk for each trade. While the earlier strategy is known as "equal-dollar weighting," this second strategy is known as *equal-risk weighting*.

Here's an example of how this risk-based position calculation would work. For the same $100,000 portfolio, let's say you are okay with a 1 percent risk per trade—meaning that you're willing to put $1,000 at risk for each position (in other words, the dollars at risk on any single trade can constitute no more than 1 percent of your total portfolio).

For the first trade that comes along, your system or strategy dictates that you will get out if the stock moves $2 against your position. Since you're willing to risk only $1,000 total on the trade, here's the math for how many shares to buy:

$1,000 (risk per trade)/$2 per share risked on this trade = 500 shares to purchase.

So that's our formula stated pretty simply, in which P = E/R, meaning:

- Equity (E) is the dollar amount to risk, divided by
- Risk (R) per share, or per contract, equals
- Position Size (P), or number of shares or contracts to buy
- Equity Chunk ($) / Risk per share ($/share) = Position size (shares)

Let's look at the math showing why equalizing your risk across trades gives you an advantage—versus just allocating equal dollar amounts across trades.

To do this comparison, we'll look at two simple accounts, each of which trades in the same two stocks.

To make this even simpler, we'll say both of the stocks trade at $50 a share.

One stock is a slow mover with very low volatility, so the stop is only $1 below the entry price. The other stock has a very high volatility, so the stop is $4 below the entry price. I'll show you exactly how to correctly set stops the 10-Minute Millionaire way in the chapters ahead. For now, however, just follow the example.

In our equal-dollar account, we'll buy $50,000 worth of each stock, or 1,000 shares. That means that we're talking about $50,000/$50 per share = 1,000 shares.

In our equal-risk account, we'll determine how many shares to buy based on risking 1 percent, or $1,000, per trade. For the stock with the $1 stop-loss, we'll buy 1,000 shares ($1,000 risk per trade/$1 risk per share = 1,000 shares). For the stock with the $4 stop-loss, we'll buy 250 shares ($1,000 risk per trade/$4 risk per share = 250 shares).

Let's look at what happens if we encounter a little bit of market weakness and the stops are hit on both stocks.

	Shares of Stock A	Shares of Stock B	Gain/(Loss) on Stock A	Gain/(Loss) on Stock B	Total Profit/ (Loss)
Dollar-Weighted Portfolio	1,000	1,000	($1,000)	($4,000)	($5,000)
Risk-Weighted Portfolio	1,000	250	($1,000)	($1,000)	($2,000)

It's easy to see that for stocks with widely varying stops, an equal-dollar portfolio can take on too much risk, especially if stocks are lower-priced and volatile.

Another scenario appears when the more volatile stock hits its stop and the less-volatile stock wins an amount twice as big as its risk or stop amount.

	Shares of Stock A	Shares of Stock B	Gain/(Loss) on Stock A	Gain/(Loss) on Stock B	Total Profit/(Loss)
Dollar-Weighted Portfolio	1,000	1,000	$2,000	($4,000)	($2,000)
Risk-Weighted Portfolio	1,000	250	$2,000	($1,000)	$1,000

In this scenario, you have one winner and one loser. In the equal-dollar portfolio, you wind up losing big. But in the equal-risk portfolio, you make money.

Without drawing a new table, you can easily see that if the both stocks move in your favor, you do make more money with the extra exposure of the equal-dollar portfolio. But *the increased profit is in equal proportion to the increased risk.*

In general, when taking on one unit of extra risk, you don't want to only get the possibility of one unit of extra return. In other words, we have no Edge.

Unconventional Wisdom

Conventional wisdom says focusing only on upside potential is the way to win—and win big—in the stock market.

As is usually the case, *conventional wisdom is wrong.*

Most folks believe that Babe Ruth swung from the heels on every pitch.

But statistics prove this wasn't the case.

The Babe was happy to hit for a high average, to get singles, doubles, and even a lot of walks—and to score lots of runs. But when he got the *right* pitch, Ruth *went* for it . . . just as he did when hammering his record sixtieth homer on that September day in 1927.

10-Minute Millionaire investors have a lot in common with the Bronx Bomber. Instead of trying to hit a homer on every trade, 10-Minute Millionaire investors swing only when they get their pitch—meaning they've identified a large Edge in the market. Edge is the ratio between the expected upside return on a trade and, more importantly, the downside risk.

$$\text{Edge} = \text{Expected return} - \text{Downside risk}$$

We find the maximum expected return when we identify stocks going to extremes (Chapter 5—Finding Extreme Stocks).

We'll minimize our downside risk using the tools of contingency exits to limit our losses on any one trade and position sizing to keep us in the game long enough to reap the reward from our Edge. (See Chapter 6—Framing the Trade.)

The 10-Minute Millionaire does lots of trades. But instead of swing-for-the-fences, make-or-break, all-or-nothing bets . . . this system specializes in identifying trades with good odds of success—just like Babe Ruth.

The parallels don't end there, either.

Although Ruth's legend portrays him as a free-swinging, all-or-nothing slugger, statistics clearly show he was much more controlled. He accepted the occasional strikeout as part of the game, but those failures were much less frequent than we see in his modern-day counterparts.

The 10-Minute Millionaire system has the same focus. There's no guarantee that each and every trade will work out, meaning there *will* be strikeouts. But the commitment to risk management . . . to keeping risk in check . . . means that, over time, you'll come out ahead—way ahead, in fact.

Babe Ruth embraced this kind of philosophy with his hitting—and was enshrined in the Baseball Hall of Fame. Similarly, if you embrace this mindset, you'll find that your career as an investor and trader will result in your coming out way, way ahead. You'll build meaningful wealth—even a millionaire's wealth.

For a Main Street investor, that's a Hall of Fame achievement.

Now it's time to show you how to get there.

We've given you the basics . . . demonstrated the fundamentals—and told you how to get a winning Edge.

The next step is to use those skills—and employ that Edge—in game conditions.

We want to show you how to win...and how to avoid the big losses...

After all, it's the human element—called emotion—that creates our profit opportunities by driving stocks and entire markets to major, exploitable extremes. But those extremes can also lead to our downfall if we're not careful, or if we engage in the same irrational behaviors that trip up the investing masses.

Next up, we'll talk about the need for trading discipline (or a trading routine) and why having a systematic approach to trading is the final key step to becoming a 10-Minute Millionaire.

Intermission

A Look Back... and a Look Ahead

My wife and I really enjoy the movies, and try to hit the theaters as often as we can. But we really enjoy settling in at home, uncorking a bottle of wine, and unwinding to a cinematic classic or new release. Because of my lifelong interest in history, I'm especially fond of classic historical fiction or period productions, and will often research a film's history—either before, or right after, we watch a show.

I remember some classics from growing up. My dad took me to watch *Tora! Tora! Tora!*—and I remember being amazed that the showing actually had an intermission (which, for a young movie-goer like me, meant there was time to grab popcorn and a soda ...).

Not that long ago, I was thinking back on some of the best times I shared with my dad and reminded him of the day. He, too, remembered the intermission. So I did some digging into the history of performance arts (plays, musicals, film screenings, and operas)—and researched the origin of the intermission.

My discovery relates to our work together here.

Intermissions—in any kind of performance—are employed for a bunch of reasons. They're a recess of sorts—a kind of break between important sections of a production. Obviously, these breaks are needed so the stagehands can change the sets, the wardrobe folks can help the actresses and actors change their costumes, and the performers can catch needed breathers.

As for the viewers... the audience... the folks being played to: for them the intermission serves as a dramatic pause. It gives the spectators a chance to think about what they've just seen and heard... and to refocus in a manner that gets them ready for the acts scheduled to follow.

This wasn't always the case, as I found from my readings.

Many years ago—back in the 1700s, to be precise—the intermission was very different. Even though there was a break in the main performance, the action didn't stop... but rather continued offstage.

Indeed, as French writer and historian Jean-Francois Marmontel wrote back in 1763: "The interval is a rest for the spectators; not for the action. The characters are deemed to continue acting during the interval from one act to another."

For me that was a scintillating bit of insight because of how it relates to what I do—which is to teach folks how to be better traders, and better investors. That's my goal when I conduct trading seminars, when I share my latest market views with my newsletter subscribers, and when I'm interviewed on TV shows.

That obviously goes triple for the work we're doing together here in *The 10-Minute Millionaire*.

And that brings me back to the history of intermissions—and *The 10-Minute Millionaire*.

I grant you... we're not on stage here—we're not performing.

But we are learning.

And we're learning about a topic (investing, trading, and wealth creation) that demands the same kind of immersive concentration we'd devote to a high-quality theatrical production.

With a play, the performers we're watching are the actors. We watch as the story unfolds. We have to think about what's happening, have to think about what it all means, and have to think about the overarching lessons... as well as considering how these lessons might be applied.

As investors, we do the very same things.

In the investing venue, of course, the performances we're concerned with are financial, not human. We watch the markets, watch individual stocks—and watch as the story they're telling us unfolds. We derive lessons from those tales, and apply what we've learned to our individual trades—and to our overarching investment strategies.

As the author of *The 10-Minute Millionaire,* I'm not performing. But I am making a presentation—complete with stories, lessons, and strategies that I want you to apply to your everyday life.

And there's a lot to absorb, I know.

Indeed, an intellectual exercise of this magnitude certainly requires an intermission... a break... to allow you to fully absorb the lessons we've already talked about. And I can aid that process by including a summary or review of what's happened so far.

But while we take this break... while we enjoy this intermission... the "action is deemed to continue"—just as Marmontel, the theater historian, wrote so many years ago.

And he's right.

Just think about it. We've spent a fair bit of time here already—talking about market extremes, about the perils of emotion-driven trading, and about the advantages of the 10-Minute Millionaire approach to the markets.

But while we take this break—while we enjoy this intermission from our production of "The 10-Minute Millionaire Investor"—the "action is deemed to continue."

In this case, however, that action that continues offstage is the trading that takes place in the financial markets all around the world... here in the United States... in Europe... and in Asia. It's the craziness that causes stocks to overrun to the upside... and to be oversold to the downside. It's the miscues that most investors repeat—over and over and over again—so that they never achieve meaningful wealth.

I love that creative way of looking at what we're doing together here.

So let's take this intermission... review what we've learned to this point... and look ahead at what's to come.

Then we'll move forward. And keep learning. And by the time we finish, you'll be ready to direct your own production.

Your production will have an exciting plot—the result of thinking that's free of conventional wisdom.

And it'll have a very happy ending—since you'll end up as a 10-Minute Millionaire.

So let's take a quick review . . . of the lessons we've learned so far.

Lesson Number 1: Time can be your biggest ally . . . or worst enemy—and the choice is yours. In this book's introduction (about Huck's Defeat) and in Chapter 1 (the 10-Minute Millionaire mindset), we learned that time is a scarce but valuable resource. And we learned that even small increments of time—as little as 10 minutes a day—can make big, big differences in your personal wealth.

Lesson Number 2: When it comes to investing, it pays to be extreme. Markets are auctions in which irrational human beings are all trying to out-game each other and make a profit. Sometimes markets get out of whack, creating extremes (Chapter 2). We can profit from those extremes and beat the markets if we learn the ways of the 10-Minute Millionaire.

Lesson Number 3: Understand the odds. Identifying out-of-whack extremes—and setting up trades that profit from those opportunities— are the end game. But that's not the entire strategy. And there are other moves you need to make to generate the steady string of winning trades and steady stream of profits that add up (over time) to true wealth, and to millionaire status. You don't want to think like a riverboat gambler who's willing to roll the dice and go for broke as he guns for that single big kill. Nor do you want to view yourself as a trader who's trying to beat the always-favored house in a game of chance. You want to BE the house by shrewdly turning probability into an ally. And you do that by establishing a true Edge (Chapter 3), which you achieve by combining the extreme profit opportunities with ironclad risk controls. When you do this, you'll win consistently, and will even string those wins together. And sometimes you'll even win big. But even when you miss, you'll miss small. In the long run, that's a combination that allows you to survive and thrive—and keeps you on the superhighway to millionaire status.

Lesson Number 4: For investors, uncontrolled emotion is Public Enemy Number 1. Even the most-carefully-conceived plans can be short-circuited by emotion. To keep this from happening, we need a system (coming up in Chapter 4) that excises emotion and maintains our Edge over time.

Now that you understand the basic framework of the 10-Minute Millionaire, it's time to flesh out the actual strategy . . . and to show you how to put it into action.

In the chapters that follow, I'll lead you through the steps to take to invest and trade like a 10-Minute Millionaire.

At the most basic level, there are three:

1. Find the Extreme (Chapter 5).
2. Frame the Trade (Chapter 6).
3. Book the Profit (Chapter 7).

Once we understand the strategy, I'll share some real-world examples of the process in action so you can see how this system actually works. And I'll demonstrate—with hard facts and real numbers—how a winning streak in the financial markets translates into steadily growing wealth.

Before long, you'll find that the 10-Minute Millionaire system has become second nature to you.

With these revelations, intermission is over.

Let's get back to the action...

SECTION II

Find the Extreme, Frame the Trade, Book the Profit

CHAPTER 4

Running a System

I value self-discipline, but creating systems that make it next to impossible to misbehave is more reliable than self-control.
                                        —Tim Ferriss, author and angel investor

Every time I read this quote, I have the exact same reaction. Tim Ferriss—an author, investor, and an advisor to companies like Facebook, Twitter, Evernote, and Uber, among others—has it right. Human emotions open the door to miscues that only a system approach can thwart.

In fact, that quote reminds me of one of my favorite bits of trading wisdom—one espoused back in 400 B.C. by Chuang Tzu, who, along with Lao Tzu, is a defining figure in Chinese Taoism.

In my investing seminars, and in talks I give to investment groups, I make a lot of my key points by using stories about risk and risk management that listeners can relate to. And if you've spent any time at all in the markets—meaning you've seen how easy it is for emotions to blur your thoughts—you'll be able to relate to my 2,400-year-old trading lesson.

> When an archer is shooting for nothing . . . he has all his skill.
> If he shoots for a brass buckle . . . he is already nervous.
> If he shoots for a prize of gold . . . he goes blind,
> Or sees two targets . . . he is out of his mind!
> His skill has not changed. But the prize . . . divides him. He cares.
> He thinks more of winning than of shooting . . .
> And the need to win drains him of power.

Chuang Tzu's message is clear . . .

In pressure situations, we all too often see *emotion* trump skill . . . trump knowledge . . . trump experience.

Two thousand years later, the same holds true in the global capital markets.

As investors . . . or as traders . . . we're financial archers. And our goal, of course, is to win gold in the form of market-beating profits.

For us here, the big prize we're shooting for is millionaire status. Or more.

So we all have a goal. We're all intelligent people. And we all have insights, knowledge, and experience gained from *years* in school, in the business world, and even in the markets.

But I'm willing to bet that one thing has blocked you from achieving that big goal . . . that gold ring prize . . . that millionaire status that I just referred to.

And it's the same obstacle that kept Chuang Tzu's archer from winning his brass buckle . . . or his prize of gold.

I'm talking, of course, about *emotion*.

With a learned skill like archery, there's no real way to systematize the process of firing an arrow into a target.

Which is why machine guns were invented.

But with investing, you *can* create a system that will blunt emotion . . . and do so in a way that removes the chaos-triggering miscues from the trading process.

Wall Street pros refer to this as "running a system."

In this chapter, I'm going to show you how to do it.

Just Enough to Be Dangerous

During my days as a chemical engineer at DuPont, whenever a colleague was first promoted to a general management position, we jokingly predicted exactly how they'd spend their first couple of weeks on the job—even if we knew nothing about them beforehand. Armed only with their previous job title, we could predict exactly where this newly promoted neophyte would be—and could also predict exactly what they'd be doing.

Accountants spent those first few weeks in their new post behind closed doors studying the numbers.

Engineers walked the plant floor examining the production line.

Salespeople went out to meet key customers.

Information technologists toured the server room and went over the IT architecture.

During periods of transition or challenge—without fail—we gravitate toward our natural biases... toward our comfort zones. It's human nature.

When I start to explain this systems approach to trading, I often think back to those DuPont days. Today, as a trader, I would never put money at risk without first having in hand a robust system to deliver safe, consistent profits. Back then, I would never attempt to synthesize complex chemicals without a proven process and a checklist to follow.

In my talks with investors, my favorite analogy is the mixing of ammonium perchlorate (AP)—which you might know by another name.

Like rocket fuel.

AP is a truly *amazing* propellant.

At room temperature, it's a solid crystalline compound. And unlike other explosives—such as nitroglycerine—it's surprisingly stable. You can drop it, kick it, or smash it—with no ill effects whatsoever.

And when it burns, it doesn't even produce smoke.

AP is safe enough for amateur model rocketeers to buy in prepackaged cartridges at Hobby Lobby. But it's powerful enough to lift the 4.4 million pounds of Space Shuttle, external tank, fuel, and solid-rocket boosters off the launch pad, and push it into orbit.

Sometimes that allure—that mix of power and apparent safety—is too compelling to ignore…and amateur rocket builders try to mix up their own batch of AP at home. The ingredients—household chemicals like table salt, ammonia, and common pool cleaner—are readily available.

However, the synthesis is anything but simple.

For starters, the anode and cathode materials for the initial oxidization stage of the process must be compatible with each other and carefully chosen. Quantities and proportions of component chemicals must be of specific concentrations measured accurately down to the hundredth of a gram.

Temperatures must be precisely controlled to within one degree and run through a gradual 24-hour cooling period on a pre-calculated gradient to ensure proper precipitation of the end product.

Any error along the way can allow powerful and highly unstable contaminants to become part of the mix. In one set of chemical ratios, those can result in a useless, harmless glop. But in a different ratio—this turns into a miscue that goes by the acronym "B.O.O.M."

As we travel this journey together, we'll repeatedly refer to the structural framework of the 10-Minute Millionaire system: identify the extreme, get an Edge, run the system.

Once you do understand this framework, you'll have the insights you need to run through the actual three-step process for making money: Find the Extreme, Frame the Trade, and Book the Profit.

We've already talked about finding the extreme and getting an Edge (and we'll circle back on both yet again).

But now it's time to focus on the last piece of this triad—running the system.

For an aspiring millionaire, knowing how to spot extremes and get an Edge—but not knowing how to run the system—is akin to saying, "Hey, I've got some household chemicals—and a rocket I really want to launch. Let's mix up this stuff and make us some *rocket fuel*. Launch comes directly after lunch."

With a proven system to guide you through the propellant-making process—while keeping you safe—you're likely to end up with one of two results at opposite ends of the spectrum.

At one end, you'll end up with a powerful propellant—one that will launch your profit rocket skyward.

At the other extreme, you'll end up with a manageable loss akin to useless sludge. Useless…but also relatively harmless. You won't be able to launch your rocket. But you also won't face the risk of blowing yourself up.

Unfortunately, if you don't have a system to guide you, you can't be sure which outcome you'll end up with. Without a system to bring uniformity, you'll get variability. You'll get careless. You'll get impatient. You'll cut corners or simply forget your recipe. You'll have no checks or balances. One bad decision will lead to more bad decisions and cascade out of control in a cataclysmic chain of failures.

At some point, you won't end up with the harmless sludge . . . or the stable high-performing propellant.

You'll end up with something in between . . . something dangerous.

That's exactly what happened back in May 1988 at the Pacific Engineering and Production Company of Nevada (PEPCON) plant, about 10 miles outside Las Vegas.

Due to a chain of human errors, ammonium perchlorate propellant intended to launch the Space Shuttle and fire Patriot missiles exploded. The series of seven blasts killed two, injured 372 others, and caused $100 million ($200 million in today's dollars) worth of property damage in a 10-mile radius around the plant. The explosive power was estimated at one kiloton—about the same as a tactical nuke.

The disaster was so violent, in fact, that the biggest of the blasts actually registered 3.5 on the Richter scale.

Without a proper trading system to guide you . . . you risk winding up inside the blast zone of your personal financial PEPCON. That's because a trading strategy that lacks a proper system for managing money and managing risk can be just as explosive as rocket fuel. The detonation will blast away your investment capital. And it will obliterate your future—and worse, your dreams.

Now that I've got your attention, let me share a story that illustrates just such a personal PEPCON—and the traffic aftermath.

The Tragic Tale of "Trader Tom"

It was December 2000, and—in addition to other services—a business partner and I were running a coaching service for investors interested in becoming more active traders.

A businessman we'll call Tom—though that's not his real name—called seeking insights on a big investment that was turning against him. Even though we're using a pseudonym, every other detail about this story is true.

Tom had spent years building and running a small business. In the late 1990s, he sold his company—at a very nice price.

As I'm sure you'll remember, this was the peak of the business cycle—making it a great time to sell a little venture at its maximum value.

It also seemed to be a great time to invest in stocks—especially Internet-related technology shares.

Like so many other folks at the time, Tom was seduced by the apparent rule-defying "it's different this time" investment opportunities that were popping up wherever you looked. In 1999 and 2000—like those other folks—Tom started day-trading tech and Internet stocks—in pursuit of the easy money everyone seemed to be talking about.

In September 2000, Tom bought what he later described as a "large quantity" of shares (he never told me how many) in chipmaker Rambus Inc. (Nasdaq: RMBS) for about $85 apiece. He intended to flip the shares for a quick profit before that same trading day ended.

At that time, Rambus seemed to be the perfect day-trading stock. It was about as volatile as could be, with an intraday trading range of $5 or $6 a share.

Tom was shooting for a fast five-figure profit—and believed he could pull it off.

As Tom saw it, the ingredients for a quick, winning trade appeared to be present. Thanks to the human emotion that had driven the dot-com feeding frenzy and was now creating volatile price movements during the early stages of the dot-com bubble bursting, U.S. stocks as a group were exhibiting definite extreme behavior. And Rambus, specifically, was experiencing a strong uptrend, rebounding from its August lows.

So, in Tom's mind, the probability of gaining an Edge on a well-structured trade seemed to be pretty high.

Unfortunately, Tom had no system—as we discovered in the talks that would follow. Tom was flying by the seat of his pants, guided by nothing more than the primal emotions of greed and fear. He'd enacted no safety provisions, and had no system for managing risk.

And without a system—in an environment as risk-laden as the dot-com era—Tom was mixing a volatile home brew . . . and risking an explosion.

When Rambus shares didn't move the way he expected—meaning it *wasn't* a one-day, big-profit trade—Tom didn't take his loss and move on in search of a new opportunity . . . which is what he should have done.

Instead, he decided to stay in the trade a little longer.

That's where my partner and I came into the picture. By December, Tom found his situation to be so uncomfortable that he telephoned and asked if we provided coaching services.

We told him that we did. After the standard intake questioning, Tom said that he had a trade that was giving him difficulty. I reminded him that we couldn't give personal financial advice, but said I could provide general guidance on what any trader should do when stuck in a bad trade. So he told me the general gist of his Rambus trade—including the missteps to date—and asked one simple question: "What should I do?"

Even though I wasn't permitted to give him personal financial advice—and I didn't—I could coach him on the general practices that any trader should follow. And that was easy: "Sell now and start fresh," was my immediate reply.

But Tom just couldn't let go. He lacked a system that would have *forced* him to do so. And his emotions wouldn't *let* him.

Over the next several months, the four of us (Tom, my partner, me . . . and Rambus) fell into a familiar (otherworldly) routine.

Rambus kept falling.

Tom kept calling.

He kept asking the same question: "What should I do?"

And he kept ignoring my counsel—the same suggestions I would make to anyone who is hanging on to a trade gone bad.

At one point, hoping to shatter this pattern, I even suggested that Tom sell a single Rambus share. My hope was that this one simple act might break Tom's emotional logjam.

Tom wouldn't even do that—proving to me that all rational thought had left him.

While I initially believed Tom truly wanted our coaching services, I quickly realized he was actually seeking a sympathetic ear—a sounding board to keep him grounded.

But he didn't want to hear what we had to say.

Tom was a smart guy, and a savvy businessman. He had all the information he needed to make the correct move. But when it came to this particular trade, emotion was trumping logic. Tom had no system to guide him—even as the stock he bought months ago to flip on the same day for a quick profit continued to fall.

On March 16, 2001, Tom telephoned for the final time.

I remember it was a Friday . . . indeed, I remember so many details of that day—including the conversation. Tom's voice was eerily steady, and each spoken syllable sounded forced, and strangely clipped.

Tom's voice may have been steady. But his words conveyed full-blown panic.

Rambus had been skidding for months. But then it plunged—losing more than half its remaining value in just two days.

The stock he'd paid $85 a share for just six months before was now trading below $16.

Tom's position was now down more than 80 percent.

And this already sad story didn't end there.

It got worse.

There was no intermission here . . . no break from the action.

Indeed, this sad saga turned into a truly tragic tale.

Instead of merely riding his original position (which I estimated to be several thousand shares) into financial oblivion, Tom actually bought *more* Rambus shares as the stock careened downward.

His *hope* was that by averaging down, he could lower the average price on his overall position, allowing him to exit his Rambus trade at breakeven—if and when the stock rebounded.

But what Tom *actually* did by adding these other shares was to transform a really big, really painful loss into one that was massive—and nearly fatal from a financial standpoint.

And this all happened because Tom *lacked a system* that made sure he would shove emotion to the sidelines and manage his trades dispassionately.

Going back to our AP rocket fuel example, it was like Tom took what was supposed to be a kitchen-table hobby experiment—and turned it into a personal PEPCON.

Heck, he even volunteered to light the match.

Tom finally pulled the ripcord on his Rambus trade. And though I didn't know the precise number of shares he was trading, I estimated his loss at roughly $400,000 ($560,000 in today's money).

Just think about that... $400,000 ...

We're talking about a block of cash that took a lifetime of work for Tom to earn and save. It very likely accounted for a majority of his trading capital.

And now it was gone—incinerated—just because Tom lacked a system for managing his trades, and managing his risk.

This is a painful story. It's also a very personal story because we've given it a human face by introducing you to the investor involved.

But this is just one story. And the reality is that investors get burned like this each and every day—over and over and over again. Investors— let's call them "people," since that's what we're really talking about here— make irrational decisions at market stretch points... and push prices up or down much more than the underlying fundamentals actually warrant.

This irrationality in the markets is a double-edged sword.

People who take the wrong sides of these trades, who trade irrationally, get hurt.

But those moments of irrationality also represent opportunities— big opportunities, in fact—for investors who are willing to understand what's really happening... and adjust their trading accordingly.

That's what this whole book is about.

It's about identifying and profiting from these opportunities.

But it's also about guarding against the irrationality in ourselves.

In the 10-Minute Millionaire approach to trading, that's what running the system is all about.

The Systematic Investor

The ugly truth is that human beings just aren't wired to be good traders.

It doesn't come naturally.

Even in our most cogent, most logical moments, our brains simply can't process the massive number of inputs required to make completely informed, completely emotion-free decisions. So we rely on shortcuts, rules of thumb, or heuristics (some of which we'll illustrate shortly).

This should come as no surprise.

Doing complex math didn't help our ancestors survive on the African savanna, Eurasian steppes, Arctic tundra, or European peaks. So-called fight-or-flight instinct has been our key response mechanism for most of human history.

Most of the time, that's a good thing—even a great thing. We're products of our ancestors' hard-wired reflexes to survive and thrive.

But such primitive responses aren't suited to many aspects of modern life.

Our ancestors would look at our twenty-first-century world as a highly unnatural environment. Most of us rely on constant external support just to get through our day. Alarm clocks wake us up each morning. Our phones and computers remind us of scheduled appointments. Global positioning satellites guide us to our destination. Guardrails and collision avoidance systems keep us from killing ourselves as we motor to and from work. Graphs, charts, and spreadsheets transform gigabytes of complex data into visualizations we can grasp and use.

These are not shameful crutches. Just the opposite, in fact. While they are mandated by our all-too-human limitations, they also illustrate our ingenuity—our ability to adapt and innovate.

In the world of trading, with its ever-increasing complexity, a system plays that very role. It acknowledges our profit-blunting (indeed, our loss-enhancing) emotions. But a system is also an innovative adaptation—a powerful enabler that helps us achieve far more than we ever could with our limited corporeal capacities.

In short, in the world of trading, a well-crafted system can:

- Act as a so-called force multiplier—serving as a proxy for an employee you can trust to mind the store while you're doing other things (one reason we can legitimately call this a 10-Minute Millionaire system...since it keeps functioning even when you're not standing right there).
- Help us make sense during periods of market confusion and force aside emotions that keep us from making logical, rational, trading decisions.
- And act as a safety net, by telling us when we need to cut our losses short.

There are other benefits, too—and in Bonus Chapter 4A, I'll detail them all.

The system I'm going to describe and help you build during the next three chapters is *your* system. It's designed to insulate you from the three main flaws (biases) in human nature that lead to 90 percent of trading failures.

It's important to know and understand these biases—so let's look at them here:

- Bias Number 1: Loss Aversion Bias (aka "The Need to Be Right"). In virtually every field, we're taught how important it is to be right—and are told over and over to avoid mistakes (especially in technical professions like medicine, engineering, or rocket science, where lives are on the line). 10-Minute Millionaire traders take a slightly different view—one that allows us to overcome this bias. We understand the probabilities and actually expect to be wrong, meaning we'll incur losses on some percentage of our trades. But we accept that—and with good reason. You see, we know that in the long run, our system will make sure that we're right more often than we're wrong. And on those trades in which we are wrong and incur losses, the risk-management pieces of our system will make sure that we lose small. In short, we know that our system will keep small losses from becoming bigger losses. And this knowledge inoculates us from the loss aversion bias.

- Bias Number 2: Streak Bias. If you've ever gazed at a cloud—and spotted familiar shapes or objects—then you know how easy it is for the human brain to detect patterns... even when those patterns don't actually exist. Traders are susceptible to streak bias—the belief that streaks should be short instead of realizing that winning or losing streaks can go on for longer than we think is logical. This bias makes us think that a small series of losing trades are a sign of continued failure. As a result, they'll often abandon trading systems that are perfectly good (and often just before that system starts to work again). The 10-Minute Millionaire system recognizes that these streaks are just random noise—and dismisses them as such. That keeps the user focused, meaning he or she will stay in the game and still be present when the next string of winners begins anew.

• Bias Number 3: Results-Orientation Bias. We've been taught all our lives that focusing on results is the way to get what we want. Our coaches, our teachers, our parents, and our bosses drill into us such messages as "winning is everything" and "nothing matters but a win." In trading, we won't always win in the short run and this can make us feel like failures. The 10-Minute Millionaire focuses on the process of our moneymaking system. We don't worry about a few trades that don't go our way. We know these losing trades are going to happen and we're prepared for that reality. We'll have enough high-quality trades to make up for them.

Now let's look at each of these three biases in more detail.

Bias Number 1: Loss Aversion Bias

Back in school, when I was studying to be a chemical engineer (a "Chem-E" in the lexicon of the business), I was told over and over that "when a doctor makes a mistake, he or she fills a coffin; but when an engineer makes a mistake, he or she fills a graveyard."

This is a great aphorism for life-or-death professions like firefighting or nuclear engineering. It's also a concept born of the Industrial Revolution. Science and technology, and machines and chemicals, have magnified the potential productive gains that a single individual can generate. These innovations have also magnified the damage that one individual can wreak—with a single mistake.

The fear of damage we can cause by that single mistake is what scientists and psychologists term "loss aversion."

The fact is that human beings hate losses *more* than they love gains. It's something that can actually be quantified.

During decades of research, experiment after experiment has consistently shown that human beings prefer avoiding losses about twice as much as they favor acquiring gains.

In one example, a group of workers were each given a $25 cash bonus at the beginning of their shift and told they could keep it if certain productivity goals were hit.[1]

Otherwise, the boss would take it away.

Nobel Prize Thoughts on Loss Aversion Bias

Daniel Kahneman shared the 2002 Nobel Prize in Economic Sciences for his work on how people make choices that involve risk. His 1979 paper written with Amos Tversky created a new behavioral economic theory call "Prospect Theory." It challenged the EMH orthodoxy by showing irrational behavior at work.

No section on loss aversion biases would be complete without a tip of the hat to the men who quantified, popularized, and legitimized the theory.

A second group of workers was told they could each earn the same $25 bonus at the end of the shift if the same productivity targets were achieved.

The outcomes in both cases were guaranteed to be exactly the same. The only difference is the starting point for each group. Group Number 1 members faced a loss of $25 for failing to achieve their goals. Group Number 2 stood to gain the same amount for the same results. In both cases, if the group hit their targets, they'd each go home with an extra $25. If not, no bonus.

Rationally, both groups should work just as hard to get the extra cash. After all, $25 is at stake regardless.

As it turns out, however, the real-world outcomes are quite different.

Group Number 1 tends to work twice as hard to avoid the loss as Group Number 2 works to get the gain—just as the theory of loss aversion bias would predict.

Let's take another example in two parts to further illustrate these strange-but-interesting manifestations in the human psyche.

In Scenario Number 1 of this experiment, imagine I just gave you $10 with the following two choices:

1. Do nothing. I'll give you an additional $5 for a total of $15.
2. Flip a coin. If the coin comes up heads, you win another $10. But if the coin lands on tails, you get nothing more (that is, you keep the original $10).

If you do nothing, you are certain to walk away with $15. If you choose to flip the coin, you have a 50/50 chance of ending up with either $10 or $20. Which option would you choose?

If you're like most folks, you'll choose to stand pat and take the sure thing $5 windfall. After all, why risk losing the guaranteed $5 for a chance at a $10 gain? Now suppose I pose the same experiment in a different way.

In Scenario Number 2, you start out with $20 and two similar choices:

1. Do nothing. I'll take away $5, leaving you with a total of $15.
2. Flip a coin. If the coin comes up heads, you lose nothing (that is, you keep your $20). But if the coin lands on tails, you lose $10.

This is the exact same decision tree as Scenario Number 1 mentioned earlier. If you do nothing, you are certain to walk away with $15. If you choose to flip the coin, you have a 50/50 chance of ending up with either $10 or $20. Which option would you choose this time?

If you're like most people, you choose to flip the coin—the exact opposite choice as Scenario Number 1 for the exact same outcome.

Visually, it looks something like what's shown in Figure 4.1.

Take a moment to think about this. It's really quite astonishing.

For a computer operating on pure logic, it's all the same math. The outcomes of any choice are exactly the same regardless of the starting point. In fact, even in the case of a coin flip, my expected return is still the same $15 as my guaranteed payout option (50 percent × $10 + 50 percent × $20 = $15). The computer would say that all choices are equal—especially over multiple trials of the experiment.

Put this into a human brain and logic gives way to emotions and mental framing.

Start:	$20.00			Start:	$10.00		
Choice:	Do Nothing	Flip Coin		Choice:	Do Nothing	Flip Coin	
Outcome:	$15.00	$20.00	$10.00	Outcome:	$15.00	$20.00	$10.00
Odds:	100%	50%	50%	Odds:	100%	50%	50%
Rationale:	Avoid guaranteed $5.00 "loss"	Take 50% chance to avoid $10.00 "loss"		Rationale:	Take guaranteed $5.00 "gain"	Forgo 50% chance at $10.00 "gain"	

Figure 4.1 Loss Aversion Bias

The subjects in Scenario Number 1 start with $10. So the status quo (doing nothing) feels like a gain of $5. By flipping a coin, they risk losing their small gain in exchange for a bigger gain. So they avoid that choice.

This is the exact same rationale traders use when they cut their gains short by selling a stock for a small profit rather than risk dropping back to breakeven even if there's a good probability for a bigger gain.

Subjects in Scenario Number 2 start with $20. So the status quo (that is, doing nothing) feels like a guaranteed loss of $5. They'd rather risk an even bigger loss for a chance to stay at their perceived breakeven point.

This is exactly what traders do when they let their losses ride. When a position moves against them, instead of getting out at a predetermined stop point, their natural human aversion to actually realizing (locking in) that loss causes them to hang on to the loser, hoping it will turn around. That perfectly describes Tom in my coaching story.

What's fascinating to me is that when this is put into a mathematical context, the starting position is completely irrelevant to our current decision. Regardless of past events, the options we have in front of us right now are entirely identical. Yet it's the perception of our past starting point that drives actual human behavior and our resulting choices.

If there's a better window directly into the human brain, I have yet to find one.

This illogic plays out each and every day in the markets.

I can't tell you how many times I've heard a student trader in a losing position say something like: "Yeah, but it's just a paper loss... and it'll rebound."

In other words, as long it's just a "paper loss" (that is, on their brokerage statement), it's not yet real. In their mind, there's still a chance for a rebound (however improbable that rebound actually might be). But once you cash out—actually book the loss—that loss is locked in... it's official.

And investors do all they can to avoid that feeling... that finality.

That's loss aversion bias.

The better question to ask—the query that (sometimes) snaps us out of this bias—is, "If you didn't own this stock, but saw it on this downtrend today, would you buy it?" The answer—as we see with the participants in Scenario Number 1 of the coin-flip experiment—is almost always "no."

Likewise, loss aversion all too often causes traders to take profits too quickly. For example, you'll have a position that suddenly bursts a bit into the black after a long stretch gyrating above/below/and above the breakeven point . . . or that's been slightly in the red, and then suddenly rallies into profitable territory. Traders who fear losses more than they value gains will grab that sudden, small windfall to feel good about their win—not stopping to fully analyze and understand that this was a trade that had lots more room to run.

The 10-Minute Millionaire system teaches you how to overcome this inherent loss aversion bias. With this system, you'll follow the Golden Rule of Trading . . . cutting your losses short while letting your profits run. You'll discover that you can be wrong in the markets— and incur occasional small losses—and still end up making a ton of money.

Even become wealthy.

Let's now turn to the second bias that my trading system will help you overcome.

Bias Number 2: Streak Bias

Here's a quick "thought exercise" for you. Say I just stepped behind a curtain, and then flipped a coin six times in a row. I reported out three sets of results as follows (where H stands for heads, and T represents tails):

1. H-T-H-T-T-H
2. H-H-H-T-T-T
3. H-H-H-H-H-H

Then I tell you that *one* was the actual result of the coin toss trial. The other two? Well, I made them up. Which result do you think is most likely to be the real one?

If you answered Result Number 1, you've got lots of company. That's how most people respond to this question. Coin tosses, by definition, are random. Result Number 1 *seems* more random than the others. Heads and tails alternate (more or less), which is internally consistent with our concept of 50/50 odds.

A streak of three heads in a row (Result Number 2) seems less likely. Flipping six heads in a row (Result Number 3) seems completely impossible.

Here's the stunner . . .

Each of these three scenarios has an equal chance of happening.

By that I mean that each of the three has the same probability of occurring—exactly one chance in 64.

If you don't believe me, check the math. Each coin has a 50 percent chance of coming up heads or tails. So over six tosses, there are precisely 64 possible combinations of results given by the equation:

$$1 \div \left(\tfrac{1}{2} \times \tfrac{1}{2} \times \tfrac{1}{2} \times \tfrac{1}{2} \times \tfrac{1}{2} \times \tfrac{1}{2} \right) = 64$$

Go ahead. Break out your calculator and run the numbers.

If this seems absurd, you now know firsthand why so many traders fall prey to streak bias. The human brain is great at seeing patterns—especially in small samples of data. And we're *terrible* at calculating probabilities.

To better see what I'm saying, let's transform Heads to Wins and Tails to Losses. When faced with a short string of losing trades (for example, L-L-L-L-L-L), most traders react in one of the two following ways:

- They might look at this small string of losers—and conclude that it's evidence of a flawed approach to the markets . . . to trading. So they dump their system—to try something else. (And they too often do this just before their system starts to work again.)
- Or they might assume that the trend is bound to reverse on the next trade or regress toward the mean (something called the "gambler's fallacy"). They might fudge their system, risking more and more on each successive trade—perhaps even eliminating their contingency stops, hoping that this so-called trend will reverse itself.

Both of these reactions are mistakes.

Really big mistakes.

Streaks (both winning streaks and losing streaks) can occur more often and persist for longer stretches than reason would dictate. We need to do lots of trades with good Edge to realize consistent long-term gains. Quitting every system or strategy at the first sign of drawdown is without question a formula for disaster. You quit when you're down and you're never around to benefit from the rebound.

Furthermore, past trades (wins or losses) have no memory.

In other words, each new flip is a new event.

So just because you experienced a recent string of losses (or bad coin flips), doesn't mean you're due for a reversal. A coin flip still has a 50/50 chance of coming up heads even after a streak of six tails in a row.

Just as we covered in our section on gaining an Edge, random results aren't always evenly balanced in the short term. If I ran 64 trials of the six-coin flip experiment—and averaged the total number of heads and tails across all of those trials—I'd probably be way closer to 50/50. I may still have some streaks of six heads (or six tails) in succession. In fact, I'd *expect* streaks like that over the course of many random trials. What would really be freaky is if every trial alternated heads-tails, head-tails—yet that's what many of us wrongly expect.

The 10-Minute Millionaire trader understands that any system needs time to achieve its expected results—its anticipated objectives. That means you need to see the results of dozens of trades—perhaps even hundreds of trades. The system I'll show you has a proven performance record over time. It's got a positive Edge. You must be mentally prepared to trade through the rough spots—you must expect them, and accept them—in order to realize that meaningful Edge.

Bias Number 3: Results-Orientation Bias

The mid-1970s seemed to be the golden age of door-to-door selling. At a time when a lot of moms still didn't work outside the home—before the Internet, cable television, or even sophisticated telemarketing—it seemed like roaming salesmen (other than the Avon ladies, these roaming sales folks were all men back then) were a regular part of the scenery in my quiet Virginia neighborhood.

These guys ranged from the benign college kids peddling encyclopedias to smooth talking "tin men" selling aluminum siding. And they included some seriously hardcore vacuum cleaner salesmen who'd throw dirt on your floor just to get your attention. Most of them used tried-and-true, old-school approaches to get that signature on the dotted line.

The families in my neighborhood were mostly middle-class working folks who looked after one another and were generally open and friendly. Being kind to strangers was viewed as Southern hospitality; the sales guys knew this and used it to their serious advantage. Once a peddler got his foot in the door—and I mean that literally—you had to watch out: you were in for a roller coaster ride of psychological and emotional maneuvering with a single goal—to separate you from your money.

These guys didn't care a whit about the financial health of their quarry, or whether their chosen "target" really needed the product or not. For the peddler, every contact was a potential sale—a mark to be "closed" through any means necessary. Empathy, guilt, flattery, intimidation, and pure attrition were all parts of the toolkit.

Once in the door, pitches could last for hours. A.B.C. stood for "always be closing." Salesmen believed they could sell anything to anyone through the art of persuasion. The 1970s sales culture was so raw it inspired the play and subsequent movie *Glengarry Glen Ross* by David Mamet that won a Pulitzer Prize in 1984.

When I was about 12, our Boy Scout troop launched a fundraiser in which each of us was given a sales quota for candy bars. Our guidance was a lighter version of the 1970s salesmen's creed.

Knock on doors.

Be persuasive.

Never take "no" for an answer.

Being a high achiever and not wanting to let the group down, I tried my best to emulate the professionals I'd watched through the years. I needed to sell 25 candy bars, so I figured I'd knock on 25 doors, sell a candy bar at each and every stop, and be done with the project.

Donning my uniform one fall evening, I went to work. The first few sales were easy. These were next-door neighbors who knew me already. They didn't really need any candy but figured they'd help out a kid that they knew.

As I got farther away from home, sales got tougher. I tried everything I could to get folks to buy. I sold the benefits ("think how much your kids will enjoy this candy"). I tried to overcome objections with a version of the "puppy dog close." ("No change? No problem. Take the candy now and I'll come back tomorrow to collect.")

I'd spend 30 minutes talking to an elderly spinster only to find she didn't have any money to spare.

I sold a few candy bars, but mostly felt rejected. I began to dread the next door—just imagining how much worse I'd feel after hearing another "no." I ended that first night with my head—and my spirits—hanging low.

I headed home feeling like a failure.

After a few days of stewing and feeling down on myself, my problem-solving instinct kicked in and I realized I was looking at this all wrong. Instead of focusing on the rejections, I needed to focus on the numbers. For every five doors I knocked on, four would answer. Of the four, one would buy a candy bar.

From then on, that's how I worked. With 15 candy bars left to sell—and a 1 in 5 knock-to-sale ratio—I knew that I needed to knock on 75 doors to get the job done. It seemed like a hefty task, but I figured if I could hit 25 a night, I could reach my sales quota with three nights of work.

My next candy sale outing was an emotional epiphany. Each "no" got me one closer to a "yes." I knew my numbers and trusted my approach—my "system." This was no longer a chore. I was just working my system. If someone wasn't interested, I'd quickly and politely move on to the next door with a smile.

Freed from the mental obligation to win every time—to "close" every single household—I found I was having fun. Lots of fun, in fact. I had a spring in my step and my new upbeat attitude must have showed. I started racking up sales, and I didn't let up. My focus was knocking on doors. The candy sales were an offshoot of *doing things right*—of sticking to my system.

In short, I had shifted from a results-oriented mindset, to a process-oriented mindset.

Pretty soon, I hit my quota.

Then I exceeded it.

In fact, I ended up with one of the top sales records that fall.

Those same traits apply to trading. It's something you *must* embrace to become a 10-Minute Millionaire.

Bad traders are like the door-to-door salesmen of decades past. They feel like they can force, cajole, guilt, or persuade every trade into a winner. Each loss is a personal failure. They hate rejection. They need to be right. So they spend way too much time anguishing over the rejections (the money-losing trades) instead of just moving on to the next opportunity.

10-Minute Millionaires understand that their system is a numbers game. The ultimate goal is still there (sell candy bars/make a million bucks in the markets). It's the *perspective* that's different. No one trade is a make-or-break proposition. Each loss gets you one trade closer to the next win. But each win isn't a reason for celebration. Gains are what we *expect*. The real goal is to gather *lots* of gains—enough, in fact, to achieve millionaire status.

To do this, *we work the system*.

We focus on executing the proper process (system) rather than obsessing over the short-term results. Because we know the results will follow.

In the goal-setting literature, there's an ongoing debate about what's most effective: setting results-oriented goals or setting process-oriented goals.

The results-oriented camp claims that a single-minded focus on a goal produces the best outcomes.

The process-oriented folks believe that an unwavering concentration on doing the right things (in short, following the process or system) will actually lead to a more consistent attainment of goals.

The 10-Minute Millionaire way is to focus on the process—the system—knowing that the results you seek will follow.

Here's why I'm telling you this.

I'm spent my career watching traders—both newcomers and veterans—so I can tell you this with a lot of confidence. So many folks who are new to trading come from a results-oriented background and try to apply that same form of goal-setting to their investments.

Unfortunately, as a newbie, that mindset can have disastrous results—as I'll demonstrate.

Let's say you have a new trader who starts out by saying, "I want to make $2,000 a month from my trades." It seems to be a modest goal, one that won't have the trader targeting overly risky opportunities.

And yet, there's still a problem here—a pretty big one, in fact.

Let's say the first month goes according to plan. Maybe even the second. But as the third month progresses, the trader looks at the calendar, looks at his or her trading account, and realizes it's the twenty-fifth of the month...and that the total (profit) so far is only $200.

The problem: the trader is $1,800 away from his or her goal...with only a few trading days left.

At this point, a results-oriented trader has three options:

1. Miss the goal (causing tremendous angst).
2. Take on more risk by making lots of unqualified (low-quality) trades—which violates the trading rules of the system.
3. Or take on more risk by bolstering (in a big way) the position size of each trade—which violates the risk-management guidelines of the system.

The first choice causes considerable stress—which can lead to the two other miscues.

The two latter choices will lead to ultimate financial disaster—perhaps not now, but eventually. There's an old investing adage that warns investors against trying to "make money you need." That maxim is usually perceived to mean "need for a house" or "need for a car." But trying to make money you "need for a goal" is just as dangerous a proposition.

And a lot of investors have blown up their accounts by making just those sorts of risky moves.

The 10-Minute Millionaire system sidesteps these risks by embracing a process-oriented focus.

In short, your goal here isn't to make a certain amount of money. The goal instead is to do things right—knowing that, if you do, you'll reap the profits you seek over the long haul.

Don't be afraid to reward yourself for doing things right. If you follow your rules and make money, give yourself an M&M.

And if you don't make money during a short stretch—but stick to your rules nevertheless—give yourself two M&Ms. That resolve—sticking with a well-designed system in the face of short-term adversity—is the very kind of commitment that will make you a winner.

In the three chapters that follow, I'm going to detail the trading process I've been referencing.

Learn the system as I show it to you. Then run the system over and over until it becomes second nature.

You must not second-guess the system. The system is already set up to succeed.

Just like my candy sales, your trading profits will be the offshoot of a well-run system.

And thanks to *The 10-Minute Millionaire,* those profit opportunities *will* come.

They'll come over time.

They'll come from the price extremes that we identify and trade—using the system I've developed for you.

BONUS CHAPTER 4A

The Five Secrets of a Sleek Trading System

Everything must be made as simple as possible. But not simpler.
—A popularized paraphrase of an Albert Einstein quote

et's face it . . . there's just something especially romantic about ships.

Indeed, if you take a spin through the history of maritime exploration, ocean travel, and naval warfare, names like *Santa Maria*, *Mayflower*, *Golden Hind*, *Victory*, *Monitor*, and *Constitution* seem to reach deep inside us . . . and strike a special emotional chord.

Even star-crossed ships—the *Titanic*, the *Lusitania*, and the *Arizona*—resonate with us on that warming, emotional level.

But as a career trader who's devoted a lifetime to the study of history—particularly military history (standard operating procedure for a trader, I assure you)—there's one name that towers above all the others.

That name is *Enterprise.*

Most of you—I'm sure—are immediately thinking of the *Starship Enterprise.*

But that's in the future—the distant future. And that means that—as far as this romance with ships is concerned—the time for the *Starship Enterprise* to be more than just a pop culture icon is still to come.

No, I'm thinking about the *Enterprise* from a past era.

From World War II.

The *U.S.S. Enterprise* (CV-6) was a U.S. Navy aircraft carrier.

A very special U.S. Navy aircraft carrier.

A *Yorktown*-class warship, the *Enterprise* was launched in 1936. And it was one of only three carriers commissioned before World War II to survive the conflict.

I have to confess: I sometimes get goose bumps when I think about this ship. It was always there when America needed her. Indeed, the *Enterprise* was involved in more Pacific actions than any other U.S. ship—including Midway, the Solomon Islands, Guadalcanal, and Leyte Gulf.

Three different times during the war the Japanese Navy proclaimed the *Enterprise* sunk—only to have to face her yet again.

Little wonder Japan referred to this aircraft carrier by another name—"The Grey Ghost."

On the home front, Americans had their own nickname for the *U.S.S. Enterprise.*

They called her the "Big E."

I love that nickname.

And I love this story.

In fact, I use it often in my investor training sessions—when I reach the point at which I'm detailing the very real benefits of a system approach to investing.

When you get right down to it, there are five very specific benefits to investment systems.

And each one is big.

I refer to them as my "Five Big E's."

Now let me show you why.

A Quintuplet of Benefits

A systems approach to investing will beat a seat-of-the-pants approach to investing any day of the week and twice on Sundays for five specific—and very definable—reasons. When trading, a system approach is superior because:

Reason Number 1: It Is *Emotionless*. On any trading journey, emotions are nice companions, but lousy guides. Investors want to believe they can make trading decisions based on facts and data—and can leave emotion out of the trading equation. But we know by the irrational nature of the financial markets (remember Fed Chair Alan Greenspan's reference to "irrational exuberance?") that investment decisions are anything but rational. That's why people get crazy and drive stocks or whole markets to extremes. One of the biggest problems I've seen with *many* traders (and especially *new* traders) is that instead of looking at the big trading picture, they treat *each trade* as a make-or-break proposition. For example, when a trade becomes a loser (even a tiny loser), instead of selling out and moving to the next opportunity, the trader holds on in hopes of a rebound. The small loss snowballs into a bigger loss. In other situations, when a trader has a small profit—but sees a small reversal—emotion drives him or her to cash out to keep the gain... even though their probability analysis shows that a *huge profit* is attainable.

> The takeaway: For the trader, a system excises emotion and allows us to approach each trade as part of a larger whole. It also helps us treat the trade from a probability standpoint. "There's a 60 percent chance of a win here, but if the 40 percent scenario plays out, and I incur a small loss, I'm okay with that because I know I can move on."

Reason Number 2: It Is *Efficient*. The essence of a system is that it lets us break a decision down into its fewest component parts. For example: *See the Pattern* ➜ *Recognize the Pattern* ➜ *Feel Good about the Pattern* ➜ *Take Action Based on the Pattern*. The result is that you spend your upfront time planning and preparing—meaning the day-to-day executions can be quick and decisive. Efficient action is at the core of the 10-Minute Millionaire. We have a system that works, meaning it takes guesswork and pondering out of our trading decisions.

The takeaway: Efficiency is the core allure of the 10-Minute Millionaire system. It's designed to help you take a small underperforming part of your money—as little as $2,500—and turn it into considerable wealth by stringing together a series of winning trades. And once you have it up and running—because it is a system—you can maintain it using very small increments of time.

Reason Number 3: It Is *Effective*. As a veteran of the capital markets, I can guarantee that practically every trader has pulled off that one blockbuster trade . . . and has been immediately seized with the thought: "How can I be certain of ever doing that again?" But a trading system gives us repeatable results—the framework to have those successes over and over again.

The takeaway: Systems let you know what to *expect*. You know that you have a higher probability of winning trades, and a lower probability of losers. You'll be able to max out your winners and cut short your losers. And you'll know what outcomes to expect as you do this day after day, week after week, year after year.

Reason Number 4: It *Eliminates* as Much Risk as Possible. Trading without risk management is like racing through a big city . . . while ignoring all the red lights: you might get away with it for a while—but it's far more likely you'll get whacked with citations and fines. And you'll eventually get into an accident—perhaps even one that's fatal. During my years in the markets, I've seen traders of all types—including "lead foots" like the devil-may-care city racer I've just described here. Traders of this ilk thumb their nose at all safety measures—and ultimately pay a steep price. But even the folks who may not view themselves as death-defying traders too often think about systematic risk management only *after* a trade goes badly against them—when it's too late.

The takeaway: Deciding whether you can afford to absorb a bigger loss—or calculating whether a position you've taken on is too big relative to the size of your trading account—isn't something you can do after the fact. A fully designed trading system includes components that minimize risk—as much as possible—before you put on a trade. And it lets you do this prudently, and without emotion.

Reason Number 5: It's *Easy* to Use. In today's volatile, news-driven markets—with the drama of global finance and the lighting rod nature of Washington always present—trading is as stressful as ever. And as risky. And as likely to ignite emotions. The answer, of course, is to embrace a trading system that blunts all those risks, but that is still simple to understand and use. Sounds like a tall order, but it really isn't.

The takeaway: Good systems simplify your trading—and your life. The 10-Minute Millionaire system makes it easy to screen for stocks that meet our requirements, makes it easy to establish parameters that put probability in our favor, and makes it easy to manage risk. Once it's up and running, it's also easy to maintain—in very small increments of time.

It's Time to Become "Truly Rich"

In my trading seminars—and with my coaching clients—I've stressed the benefits of systematic trading—what I've come to refer to as my "Five Big E's"—in creating an investing and trading system that is both user-friendly and effective in delivering the desired results.

To help folks really understand this, I often urge my audience or coaching clients to picture their system as a kind of trusted employee. This is actually quite a powerful concept, and one for which I've received great feedback over the years.

Your trading system provides many of the same benefits as a trusted associate—a person you can delegate work to…and do so with confidence.

This ability to delegate—to offload responsibilities and worries without fear—will bring you many personal benefits. By having a trusted system, you'll find that you're able to become (as much as possible) a stress-free trader. You'll discover you aren't obsessing about individual trades (wins or losses), since you've delegated that responsibility. That allows you to focus on the bigger picture—your larger financial goals.

You have more "mental RAM" available. When you have a system that you have confidence in—and as you watch your winnings (earnings) mount, you'll find that you have processing power available for some of the other challenges that await you...such as your job...your community efforts ... and perhaps some formerly unattainable personal goals that you set. But now these challenges are invigorating, even scintillating—and aren't daunting or odious. As your trading successes mount, so will the successes in other parts of your life.

When this system is up and running—and delivering consistent results—you'll suddenly realize how much more emotionally centered you've become in your life. I'm a true believer in the axiom that money can't buy you happiness. However, not having to worry about money—because you have a trusted trading system that's multiplying your assets—is calming...even soothing. You'll be heartened to discover that many other people seek your company—and not because of your net worth. They seek your company because you exude warmth and confidence—and always seem to have time for others. They'll view you as an emitter of positive energy—and you'll find that this upbeat outlook is "infecting" others in your life.

When this personal epiphany comes—as it will—you'll realize that you've made one of life's truly great discoveries: that your "being rich" is only partly due to your steadily growing capital base.

Note

1. Tanjim Hossain and John A. List, "The Behavioralist Visits the Factory: Increasing Productivity Using Simple Framing Manipulations," *Management Science* 58, no. 12 (2012).

CHAPTER 5

Finding Extreme Stocks

Part I: Fast Movers

You can play fast, but not in a hurry.

—NBA MVP Stephen Curry

A s an engineer, I've always been intrigued by airplanes. And why not? Flying machines are mechanical marvels—one of the ultimate achievements of engineering.

And during my professional career as an engineer, entrepreneur, investor, and hedge fund officer—and now, because of my frequent appearances as a TV investment analyst—I've spent a lot of time as an airplane passenger.

What this all means is that I've had lots of conversations with lots of pilots—private, commercial, corporate, and military.

And as a technically minded guy who also appreciates history and the arts, I truly understand how most pilots feel about flying.

There's the science of aviation—meaning the nuts-and-bolts technology of the airplane. Then there's the romance of flight—the feeling of freedom you get after leaving the ground... and that's reinforced when you look down to admire the patchwork pattern below.

As one of my friends—a gent who has military and private flying experience—once told me, the training that gets you ready to pilot an airplane is really broken into two distinct pieces.

There's ground school—the book-learning part of flight training.

And there's the actual, hands-on lessons.

These two pieces are very, very different.

As my buddy said in that talk years back, the book-learning came quite naturally. My friend is a technically minded guy—much like me. So the study of a technical subject like this was simple—even fun.

Then came the time for him to jump into a cockpit—to learn to actually fly a plane.

"Intellectually, because of my ground school studies, I 'knew' everything I needed to know to be an accomplished pilot," he told me. "I knew all about the pre-flight check, the radio procedures, aerial navigation, and exactly what all those dials, switches, and knobs on the instrument panel before me were supposed to do. But I needed to develop a completely separate—completely new—set of skills to bring the aircraft to life, to send it down the runway, to lift it into the sky ... and to fly it successfully and safely once I was airborne. I needed to develop a 'touch' ... instincts ... and confidence in what I was doing. It took time. And I made mistakes. It was frustrating at first. . . even shook my confidence. But my studies gave me a great foundation. I didn't take unneeded risks. I got a little better ... then I got a lot better. Then came the day when I realized that I *loved* what I was doing. Truly loved it."

This story is a lot like the start-to-finish journey you'll take on your way to becoming a successful 10-Minute Millionaire.

You need to finish ground school. Then you'll be able to get into the cockpit ... and to develop the instincts that will let you navigate the markets, fly your trades, and go wherever you wish to.

And just as my friend learned to *love* flying, you'll learn to *love* trading.

Especially when you see how *fat* your portfolio gets.

So let's get you cleared for take-off . . .

Navigating Your Way

Identifying extreme stocks—shares whose prices have been over-stretched to the upside, or to the downside—really is a lot like flying a small plane.

You've got a great vantage point—at a high altitude, looking down, which gives you the ability to see a *long way* in every direction. You can pick out identifying landmarks—landmarks that tell you exactly where you are in the price cycle that extreme stocks go through.

It sounds like a pleasant journey. And it can be.

But it can also be quite disconcerting—for, at times, there's an awful lot going on.

I mean, you're often buffeted by strong winds . . . you have to watch your fuel consumption and your oil pressure . . . you can't forget about your compass headings . . . and you must be vigilant—with your eyes constantly sweeping the skies around you to keep clear of other aircraft.

Forget about *any* of those things and, well, you're in trouble.

The same is true of trading. There are buffeting headwinds (currencies, interest rates, or bad news surprises) and helpful tailwinds (upside-earnings surprises, central bank rate cuts). There are other travelers in your air space (bearish investors and opportunistic short sellers)—all of whom you must watch out for.

You have to watch your oil pressure (amount at risk) and fuel situation (total available capital). And your compass headings (whether you are long or short on a trade). You must be mindful of your flight time (for example, the expiration dates on your options contracts). And you need to know your destination (your short-term, intermediate-term, and long-term financial goals).

Again . . . forget about *any* of those things . . . and you've got yourself a problem.

Trading is like flying in another way, too: the higher you fly, the tougher it is to identify things on the ground.

And given the fact that there are more than 45,000 stocks trading on exchanges worldwide, picking out the few that are experiencing trading extremes at any given moment can be challenging.

Just think of it this way: if each of those 45,000 stocks were one person, we'd be able to fill Alumni Stadium at Boston College to standing-room-only capacity.

That's *a lot* of stocks.

Way too many to study with meaningful precision.

Heck, if you spent just 15 seconds screening each of those stocks—hardly enough to get a real sense of its worth, upside, and risk—you'd use up a month's worth of nonstop, 40-hour workweeks.

By that time—given how fast markets move these days—whatever you learned about the stocks you studied at the beginning of that stretch would be long out of date.

Let's say we simplified things a bit, and limited our search to the 3,700 stocks listed on U.S. exchanges.

Even that minimalist 15-second screening regimen would require us to pore over stock charts and research reports for a solid two days—and once again we'd probably fail in our attempt to zero in on the truly most-promising profit candidates.

Such a cursory screening process is insanely risky ... and is hardly the 10-Minute Millionaire way.

Naturally, there's a solution.

A good one.

Like the combat planes of the modern military, we can employ technology to serve as a targeting aid.

This targeting system will help us identify the stocks that are capable of explosive moves—stocks that are able to move the fastest ... or climb the highest ... from their current trading altitude.

In the military, aircraft that are capable of such explosive surges—of that kind of blinding acceleration ... and that are able to fly to such extreme altitudes—are known as "Fast Movers."

We want to find stocks with that kind of Fast Mover potential. And we want to eliminate those that lack that breakout potential.

To focus our efforts here, I've divided this chapter into two sections.

Here in Part I, we'll be eliminating stocks from consideration based on three factors—namely: Volatility, Volume, and Price.

Tools of the Trade

Back in the old days (when I was starting out as a trader) when I wanted to get "real-time" market information—I relied on slow-to-update data on one of the first PC versions of the green-screen Quotron terminal. (If you want to see what a trading room looked like back then, watch the first half hour or so of the hit 1987 film *Wall Street*. Quotrons are prominently featured there.)

Sure, I could always find a company's stock price in the next day's *Wall Street Journal,* or scan my *Standard & Poor's Stock Guide.* By going that route, however, the data was old news when I finally perused it. The powerful software and trading-floor access that I needed to truly analyze the markets on a real-time basis was zealously guarded—protected by Wall Street's inner sanctum.

Obviously, the goal of that institutional cabal was to limit data access to maintain its hefty advantage over smaller rivals and independents like me.

These days, institution-quality trading tools are widely available (usually for a small fee) to anyone with an Internet connection. Real-time quotes . . . dynamic-charting software . . . customizable stock-screening programs. All of this powerful trading technology is easily accessible. And it makes it pretty easy to segment the markets and identify the best trading opportunities—in seconds, instead of days like before. Even with these tools—and even with the development of so-called neural networks, with the creation of artificial-intelligence (AI) enabled "black-box" trading platforms, and with the emergence of robo-trading—there's one thing you must keep in mind.

Your brain is still the most powerful weapon in your arsenal.

Almost every online trading service offers charting and screening tools as part of its service offerings. These tools will help you with all three steps in the 10-Minute Millionaire system: Find the Extreme (the trading opportunities in the market), Frame the Trade (structure the trade itself), and Book the Profit (know how far to play the trade and how to identify when it's time to get out). All the techniques I'll teach you can be used in some form or fashion with those tools.

(Continued)

(Continued)

Since I can't possibly cover all the screening and charting tools available in the marketplace today, the examples I provide in the following chapters are all from StockCharts.com. I've used and demoed dozens of tools throughout my trading career and, so far, StockCharts.com is my favorite. It's very powerful. And it's easy to use. Both qualities are hallmarks of the 10-Minute Millionaire approach.

And since it's Internet-based, it's easy for anyone to access.

The bottom line: this is a trading tool that does exactly what we need to do—quickly, and reliably.

Given my experiences, I'd suggest you start out on your path to becoming a 10-Minute Millionaire by using StockCharts.com exactly as I describe in the pages ahead. When you're just beginning, the last thing you need is an additional layer of complexity. By using the same analysis platform I detail here, you can follow my examples verbatim and eliminate the need to translate the screening and charting controls to a different user interface.

Throughout the rest of this book, I'll be using the term "StockCharts.com" as a stand-in for whatever trade-screening and charting tool you choose.

In the next section, we'll explore the "why" component of screening for stocks. But don't worry—right after that, I'll come right back and demonstrate the exact "how" to do the screening. It's simple and the system is already waiting for you.

From there, we'll be ready for Part 2 of Finding the Extreme, and will screen for "Rubber Band" stocks—Fast Mover profit plays that have been stretched to their ultimate extremes. They are so stretched, in fact, that these stocks are poised for big snapbacks.

V Is for Volatility

10-Minute Millionaires aren't buy-and-hold investors.

They're traders.

But they're not reckless traders.

That's why they can end up as millionaires.

But the trading strategy that I've crafted and am advocating here means we're intentionally going to seek out Fast Movers.

Fast Mover is an interesting term, for it has different meanings in different contexts.

But in each of those unique contexts, the term describes exactly what it's referring to.

One of those contexts is aviation, where a fast mover is a euphemism for a fast-moving, fixed-wing aircraft—usually a jet fighter.

Then there's our context—the stock market.

Here, a Fast Mover is a stock, option, or security capable of moving two, three, four, or even five times as much as key market indexes—like the Dow Jones Industrial Average (which retail investors follow) or the Standard & Poor's 500 Index (which the pros follow).

We like Fast Movers. After all, we're not out to *match* the market. We're out to *beat* the market. Even *thrash* the market, if possible.

The key measuring metric we'll employ to judge a stock's potential—and our results—is something known as "volatility."

When I'm talking to a group of non-investors about my craft, I eventually get to the part of my presentation that deals with volatility.

And once I get there, I usually share a story about a demonstration put on by my freshman year college honors chemistry professor . . . who I'll refer to here as "Dr. K."

You see, Dr. K. was the kind of prof that students really dug.

He was a showman . . . and his demonstrations were the stuff of legend.

Every year he performed to a packed house (lecture hall) of students. (Even Monsieur Marmontel, our French writer friend—and an expert on intermissions and theater performances—would've liked Dr. K.)

The chemistry prof kicked off his annual performance by wordlessly dimming the lights and placing one of those narrow-necked, five-gallon glass water bottles (the type used in water coolers until "plastics" became "the future") up on the black-countered lab table.

At that point, Dr. K. held up a small test tube filled with a clear liquid—and poured that fluid into the water bottle.

Then he swirled the jug around for a couple of seconds.

Dr. K. was famous—even infamous—for using exciting demonstrations to amplify his teachings. So by this point in his "show," he had *everyone's* attention.

All of us were leaning forward, wondering what cool surprise this teacher had in store for us this time.

Dr. K. then held up a wooden kitchen match, lit it . . . and carefully passed it across the jug's narrow opening.

After a W-H-O-O-S-H-like sound effect, super-heated blue flames erupted from that jug—eliciting a unified gasp from the class and prompting everyone (even the big football stars) to recoil in our seats . . . like you see in a theater during the scariest and most unexpected moment in a horror movie.

As the flames in the big jug danced back to darkness—winking out like a bottled fairytale pixie—Dr. K. explained the phenomenon, knowing that there were many non-science types in the standing-room-only audience.

Ordinary rubbing alcohol (isopropanol), as you've probably experienced, evaporates quickly at room temperature. In chemistry, we would say that these alcohol molecules are extremely volatile. They jump around way more than, say, water. And they quickly fill an enclosed space mixing thoroughly with atmospheric oxygen. The result is a giant surface area of reactive components that are poised to ignite with a simple catalyst . . . in this case, Dr. K's kitchen match.

Most buy-and-hold investors have been conditioned to believe that volatility of this magnitude is a bad thing . . . always. In fact, the CBOE Volatility Index (also known as the "VIX") has been nicknamed the "Fear Gauge" or "Fear Index" by the mainstream media.

Now, it's true that—with investments and chemicals alike—potentially volatile substances that are not handled correctly, and that aren't respected for their potential destructive power, can wreak havoc. They can result in a horrific carnage—including destruction and death.

But as I learned during my career as a chemical engineer, those same substances—when handled with respect, and used correctly—can also be employed to great benefit.

In industry, volatile substances—utilized in the correct manner—can drive our cars and airplanes, can heat our homes, and can power our factories. This volatility can be used to create all sorts of new products—which, in turn, create new businesses, new jobs, and meaningful wealth in our modern economy.

It's no different in the financial markets.

Find a "volatile" stock, identify the "spark" (the catalyst) to ignite it, and you can create a burst of profits . . . almost instantly.

For the 10-Minute Millionaire, volatility is a friend.

A *best* friend.

A Measured Approach

So we've learned to respect volatility. And we've now learned that volatility can be used to great advantage.

But how do we recognize volatility? And how do we measure it?

In chemistry, we do this by using an indicator called "vapor pressure." The higher the vapor pressure of a substance at any given temperature, the faster its molecules are jumping around.

In the financial markets, there's another indicator we use.

In trader slang, it's known as Average True Range, or ATR.

Many of us have been taught (mostly by the buy-and-hold proponents) that something called "beta" is the correct and only measure of volatility we need to be concerned with. A stock with a beta of 1.0 generally moves about as much as the broader market (usually the S&P 500)—and in the same direction. If the S&P 500 is up (or down) 10 percent, we'd expect a 1.0 beta stock to be up (or down) by about the same magnitude.

A stock with a beta of 2.0 is generally perceived to move twice as much as the market . . . and so on. But we'll see that this perception isn't really reality.

If you've ever picked up a kid from school at recess, you have a great mental analogy for the concept of beta. Some kids are tearing around like their hair is on fire. Others play more leisurely on swings and slides. Still others are sitting on benches, preferring to read books.

Stocks are just like these kids. Some are super-active. Others are average. And others are laid back.

A Word on Beta

Beta measures an investment's long-term correlation with the Standard & Poor's 500 Index. For our system, however, it's a poor indicator of short-term volatility. Instead of volatility or range of movement, beta actually measures the "sameness" or correlation to the S&P 500. It can help in measuring the systemic risk of a portfolio, mutual fund, or buy-and-hold stock. But be aware that lower beta stocks can still have higher volatility, and vice versa.

Some of this is innate . . . it's their nature. But there's also a situational component to this, too. You're seeing a snapshot of a single moment. Perhaps the kid who is super-active at that moment you observe him is typically sedate—except when there's a game of tag, which is the one game she loves to play.

And perhaps the boy who's reading the book is usually super-active—but you're watching him not realizing that he had a Little League game the night before . . . and has been ordered by mom to take it easy because he got beaned and is feeling sore.

How are we to know which kids have a high-energy temperament and which ones just got amped up on a short-term sugar rush? With kids, I'd probably just give each one a pedometer and take daily readings over a couple of weeks to see who typically moves around the most. That would be a useful way to see who was most active. But that's not how beta works.

Beta would compare each kid's position on the playground once a month over a three-year period and then see how different those individual readings are compared to the average activity of the entire group of kids at recess.

That type of long-term comparison to a broad average is moderately useful for measuring the systemic risk of a portfolio, mutual fund, or buy-and-hold stock.

But the 10-Minute Millionaire doesn't play by the conventional buy-and-hold rules.

Beta measures the long-term correlation of an investment with the broader market index. It's backward looking, typically comparing month-end prices over a three-year period.

That's modestly useful information, for some very-long-term port-folios.

But for the 10-Minute Millionaire, who is screening for short-term extremes, beta is a poor indicator of volatility. For our system, we want something more relevant . . . with information that's much more current.

Instead of a long-term indicator like beta—one that's been devel-oped using regression analysis—we want a metric that tells us how likely it is for a stock to move *now*.

We want a metric that tells us which stocks will experience bigger moves than the S&P 500 Index during a given time frame. One that can spotlight the stocks that will stage the biggest and fastest recoveries from out-of-whack extremes. One called Average True Range, or ATR.

The ATR indicator was originally developed by J. Welles Wilder Jr. to measure volatility in commodities—since price gaps there are com-mon. (A "price gap" is the difference between the closing price one day and the opening price the next.) ATR has proven equally useful for flagging extreme volatility in the stock market.

The concept of ranges is useful, and for one very good reason: when read correctly, they give us a viewport into the mindset of other traders in the market . . . the very folks creating the extremes that we're seeking to trade.

Ranges that are large—or that are increasing—suggest that trad-ers are getting irrational, and are willing to bid a stock up or sell it down . . . into extreme territories . . . throughout the course of the day.

In short, this gives us the precise information we're looking for.

Conversely, ATRs that are lower—or that are decreasing—signify tepid interest in a stock, or identify stocks that are behaving more rationally.

What ATR *doesn't do* is provide an indication of the price-trend direction. It simply indicates the *degree* of price volatility—which is fine by us. We'll get to directional indicators later. Right now, though, we just need to find stocks that have the best potential for making big moves—that are able to bounce back in a big way after going extreme—regard-less of their direction.

What ATR measures is the *daily range* of a stock, accounting for price gaps between trading sessions. Stocks that cover more ground each day by trading through a larger range of prices regardless of direction (like our hyperactive grade-schoolers) have a higher ATR, regardless of their long-term tendencies (that is, regardless of their beta).

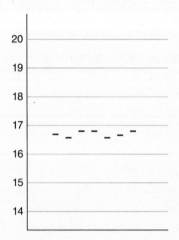

Figure 5.1 Close-to-Close Range

To see how this works, consider what would happen if we calculated a stock's trading range based solely on its closing prices (see Figure 5.1).

From this perspective, it looks like we have a low-volatility stock that only trades in a range of about a quarter point between $16.50 and $16.75. As an interesting aside, this is the data that the beta indicator uses, except it uses month-to-month closes, eliminating all the movement that happened in between. This is yet another reason why beta isn't as useful as other tools for measuring volatility.

Now look at what happens if we measure the *full* inter-day range of prices for the same stock (see Figure 5.2).

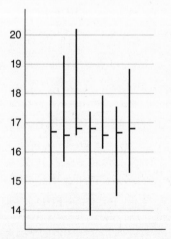

Figure 5.2 Inter-Day Range

Holy mackerel. What looked like a quarter-point sleeper turns out to be as volatile as undiluted nitroglycerine (and trust me, that's *volatile*). Including inter-day price moves (that is, how much it moved during the day between the open and close), the stock ranged more than $6 a share—from a high above $20 one day to a low below $14 the next. While that amount of volatility is unusually high, it helps show how important it is for us to understand inter-day ranges.

The True Range accounts for these inter-day movements along with one other important condition—one called "gap openings." For a closer look at this, check out my example in Figure 5.3. On Day 1, the stock in our example ranged from about $18 a share to $19. The next day, it traded between $16 and $17. If we only measured the difference between the high and low of a stock each day, we'd calculate a range of about 1 point (i.e. $19 minus $18 ... or $17 minus $16).

But what we're failing to capture is the *big gap* between the trading range *across both days*.

The True Range calculation (Figure 5.4) accounts for these missing gaps by using the largest of three volatility calculations for each trading day, namely the:

a. Current high minus the current low.
b. The current high minus the previous close (absolute value—meaning ignore any negative signs for down moves; we're capturing movement here, not direction ... that's comes later).
c. Or the current low minus the previous close (absolute value).

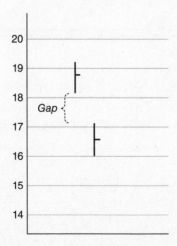

Figure 5.3   Gap Opening

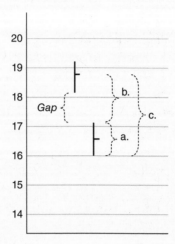

Figure 5.4 True Range

The *Average* True Range is just what its name implies: it's the simple average of our *individual* True Range calculations over a series of trading days. For purposes of the 10-Minute Millionaire—as a general rule—we'll be looking at ATR over a 14-day period ... which is just what Wilder, the indicator's creator, recommends as optimal. That's also the number that is the default value in most charting software.

ATR is a powerful tool to capture the *full* scope of short-term volatility (including often-overlooked gaps)—and to help us flag stocks that will be most explosive after hitting extremes. But we need an additional tweak to make it useful for our purposes.

This tweak is the one that has caused many pro traders and beginners alike to tell me, "Wow! That's a really excellent way to compare potential moves in stocks."

Here's why they got so excited.

Imagine a $20 stock that has a 14-day Average True Range of two points ($2 a share). Viewed strictly in dollar terms, this would appear to be twice as volatile as a $5 stock with a range of one point, right?

Not quite.

While the dollar (point) range is important, what we're really interested in is the *relative move*—the amount of the move relative to the stock's underlying share price.

As tweaks go, this one is simple.

Take the ATR divided by the current stock price and *voila!* We now have a measure of short-term volatility that we can use to compare—on an apples-to-apples basis—the stock we're analyzing with other stocks *and* with the broader market.

But what's the right ATR number? Well, all things being equal, higher seems better, right? But *how* high?

As a rule of thumb, we want to look for stocks moving at least *twice as much* as the overall market.

Since volatility ebbs and flows for individual stocks as well as for indexes, I can't give you a single number and say that it's good for all time. So here's what we'll do.

First, call up a chart on the S&P 500 Index ($SPX on StockCharts. com), or on the Nasdaq Composite Index ($COMPQ)—or on whatever index is appropriate to the market you're trading. Then add a 14-day Average True Range (ATR) indicator from the technical indicator dropdown selections. Take the current ATR and divide it by the current index price. Now double that number (multiply by two) and you'll have your threshold ATR/Price number.

Let's work through a quick example.

Let's say the S&P is trading at 2,000 with an ATR of 20. This means that the ATR for the S&P is 1 percent—which tells us that, over the last 14 trading days, the S&P's average movement each day (low to high, taking into account gaps) was about 1 percent of its price. That means my threshold would be 0.020 (that is, 20/2,000 × 2), or about 2.0 percent (see the example in Figure 5.5.)

To make it even easier, just use Step 1A on the trading worksheet included in the Appendix section at the back of this book.

Keep in mind that this is your *minimum* volatility threshold. There's nothing to say you can't include stocks with even higher volatilities. Indeed,

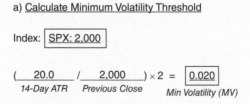

a) Calculate Minimum Volatility Threshold

Index: SPX: 2,000

(20.0 / 2,000) × 2 = 0.020
14-Day ATR   Previous Close   Min Volatility (MV)

Figure 5.5   Minimum Volatility Threshold

you should—and in most cases, the higher the better. (Coming up, in fact, I'll even show you *how* to calibrate the system for maximum volatility.)

Conversely, if the market is relatively dead—meaning only a handful of stocks are showing extreme tendencies—then just back off.

Wait a day or two.

Don't force the issue if other traders aren't feeling hyperactive.

One of the great advantages individual traders have over the Wall Street money managers is that we can choose to be out of the market when conditions are not favorable for us.

Volume and Price (How Much . . . and How High)

Okay, so we've now reached the point at which we've learned to identify volatile stocks with extreme price-movement potential.

But under the 10-Minute Millionaire regimen, that isn't *the only qualifier we need before we start looking for our trade entry.*

We need to pare the universe of stocks down some more.

Indeed, we also need to make sure the stocks we're looking at have enough volume *and* liquidity to support our trading system.

Low-volume stocks tend to have wider bid-ask spreads, a fact that makes it tougher to profit from quick moves.

The spread is the difference between the highest price that buyers are willing to pay (the bid) and the lowest price at which sellers are willing to sell (the ask).

Here's a real-world example: for a used car, the bid is the price the car dealer is willing to pay to buy a certain car; and the ask is the price at which the dealer is willing to sell. In the same way, floor traders and market makers earn their livings by pocketing the difference on every trading transaction—regardless of a stock's direction. For them, the wider the spread, the better they like it. For us, the wider the spread, the more a stock has to move before we can profit from a trade. (Figure 5.6).

		Stock A	Stock B
(Buy)	Bid	$21.09	$21.09
(Sell)	Ask	$21.11	$21.59
	Spread	$ 0.02	$ 0.50
	% Move	0.09%	2.37%

Figure 5.6 Bid-Ask Spread

Stock A in my example needs to move only two pennies a share to cover the spread, while Stock B has to go up 50 cents before a buyer at $21.09 can get out at just breakeven. All things being equal, I'm looking for narrow spreads to get the most juice (what traders refer to in Wall Street jargon as "optimal efficiency") from my trading program.

We also want to be sure that our trades get fully executed at the *right* price. With higher-volume stocks, there are plenty of buyers and plenty of sellers with enough shares in play to make sure I don't get stuck with a partially filled order.

Although it's not a hard-and-fast number, I'll eliminate any stocks that don't routinely trade more than 500,000 shares a day. And not just on a single day; I want stocks with average daily volume in excess of 500,000 over the last 14 trading days.

Finally—to be efficient—we need a filter to make sure we're trading stocks that most brokers allow. There are brokers who make a distinction between stocks that trade above $5 per share and those that trade below $5. Historically, this $5 price point is the line of demarcation for securities viewed as "penny stocks." Indeed, that $5 per share line is still part of the official Securities and Exchange Commission (SEC) definition of penny stocks.

Since we want to rule out stocks that can be difficult to trade, we'll just filter out any with trading prices of less than $5 per share.

When establishing your own share-price parameters—and especially after you become comfortable with the 10-Minute Millionaire program—you may focus on minimum dollar values that are lower or higher than those I'm recommending here. And that's fine. For now, however, we'll weed out any stocks trading at less than $5 a share.

More-seasoned traders may also use a market-capitalization filter. Generally speaking, however, if a stock has sufficient volume and a very small bid-ask spread, it can be traded efficiently.

One final note: stocks that trade on overseas exchanges can also pose some unique challenges. They're often less liquid. They may trade at different hours than you're used to (because of time zone differences). And they are sometimes not available to U.S. investors (because of ownership restrictions). In many countries, disclosure rules are a lot less stringent, making it tougher to get a real picture of a company's business and finances. All of these issues can exacerbate the risks you face.

So, at least when starting out, it makes sense to exclude non–U.S.-listed stocks, too. Thus, in the analysis that follows, we'll be sticking with U.S.-listed shares—those trading on the New York Stock Exchange (the NYSE or "Big Board"), the American Stock Exchange (AMEX), and the Nasdaq Stock Market.

Screening for Fast Movers

At this point, we're ready to do our initial screen—to whittle down our market universe into a basket of stocks with the greatest potential for a big pop after an extreme move has happened.

That means it's finally time to log in to StockCharts.com. Click the Members link at the top of the page and then navigate to the Advanced Scan Workbench. (See Figure 5.7.)

Next, enter the following code into the Scan Criteria box—exactly as shown in Figure 5.8 (where MV is your minimum volatility as calculated in Step 1A of the trading worksheet shown in the Appendix). Then click "Run Scan."

While it may seem mysterious and syntactically awkward at first, this code specifies the stock screening criteria in a language that StockCharts .com can understand. Over time, you'll get more comfortable with this scanning parlance and will be able to tweak your screening criteria; you'll even be able to create and run customized special-purpose scans to profit from unique opportunities you've identified on your own. (And when you get to that point—trust me on this—you'll experience the same emotional charge that early explorers felt as they embarked upon their own adventures long, long ago. And when these investing forays pay off, you'll feel like you've made an important new discovery.)

The result of this particular scan I've detailed here, however, will be an alphabetized list of stocks that meet all of our parameters, making them Fast Mover candidates.

As I put this book together, I ran this scan (with the same minimum volatility of 0.02 that we used in our example). It gave me a list of hundreds of stocks to choose from.

StockCharts.com - Members

Welcome

| HOME | FREE CHARTS | CHART SCHOOL | BLOGS | MARKET MESSAGE | SUPPORT | MEMBERS |

Create a Chart: SharpChart ▼ Enter Symbol or Company Name Go Symbol Catalog

Extra Control Center

This page gives you direct access to our most powerful charting tools. In addition to the charting tools listed on the right side of this page, we also have:

- **Your ChartLists** - review your saved ChartLists at the bottom of this page
- **SharpCharts Workbench** - create new bar/candlestick charts
- **Public ChartLists** - review annotated charts and commentary from other members
- **Standard Scan Workbench** - create simple technical scans via dropdowns
- **Advanced Scan Workbench** - create custom technical scans for any situation
- **Predefined Scan Results** - review results of common scans updated continually
- **Point & Figure Charting Workbench** - create the best P&F charts on the web
- **Technical Alert Workbench** - get notified whenever your specific technical situations occur
- **Technical Alert Summary** - see a concise summary of all your current technical alerts
- **User Defined Index Workbench** - upload and update your own personal index

Upgrade to PRO and get the following additional tools:

- **Quicker Auto-Refresh** - charts that auto-refresh every 5 seconds
- **Larger, Longer Charts** - 2500 pixel wide quarterly and yearly charts going back multiple decades
- **Your Own User-Defined Index** - upload and chart your own data
- **More Saved Scans and Technical Alerts** - find and get notified about more technical signals
- **Secure SSL Site Access** - encrypted transmission of your charts and annotations
- **Online Chat-based Support** - chat online with our customer support team

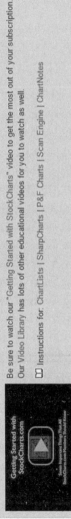

Getting Started with StockCharts.com

Be sure to watch our "Getting Started with StockCharts" video to get the most out of your subscription. Our Video Library has lots of other educational videos for you to watch as well.

☒ Instructions for: ChartLists | SharpCharts | P&F Charts | Scan Engine | ChartNotes

Figure 5.7 Launching StockCharts.com

SOURCE: Courtesy of StockCharts.com

141

```
Scan Criteria:

[type = stock]
and [Country is US]
and [SMA(14, Volume) > 500,000]
and [Close > 5.00]
and [ATR(14) / Close > MV]
```

Figure 5.8   Scan Criteria

That's way too big a list to be manageable.

If you hit days when this happens, here are a few easy adjustments you can make:

- First, increase the minimum volume requirement. By ramping this up to an average of one million shares per day, you'll eliminate some marginal stocks which generally will get even tighter bid-ask spreads.
- Second, raise your minimum price to $10—or even to $15. (If you wish, do this in incremental steps to see what you come up with at each price level). That should excise a bunch of stocks hovering right above our penny-stock threshold.
- Third, sort by the ATR/Price indicator and focus on the Top 50 or so. Otherwise, just increase your minimum volatility in the scan box to 2.5 times, three times, or even four times the market . . . and rerun the scan.

Remember, the MV indicator is a *minimum*. If you have an over-abundance of stocks to choose from, it's better to pick from only the *most* volatile.

Beginning traders can run this scan once every two weeks or so—or whenever you're ready to put on new trades. With an approach like this, we're eliminating the stocks making purely news-driven moves in order to focus on the stocks we want—those whose price movements are based on the underlying technical conditions.

And always be sure to use your judgment. The result of the scan isn't intended to be a literal shopping list. If you see some stocks you like—but they have a lower volatility than something faster-moving but more obscure—feel free to shuffle them up and make some substitutions until you get a basket of stocks that you're comfortable with.

Once you have a manageable basket of 50 stocks or so, save the list (or download it). Give it a name—something descriptive like "Fast Movers"... or something motivational like "Operation 10-Minute Millionaire" with the current date. And hold on to it: from this list you'll select the group of stocks you want for further analysis.

We'll be returning to that list in Part II when we start Finding the Extremes.

Part II: Rubber Band Stocks

Some people were like rubber bands—willing to stretch but eager to snap back into place at the first opportunity.
                                                    —Mystery writer Stephanie Bond

Kids have a natural fascination with rubber bands. When I was little, they served as a proxy for artillery shells in the games we used to play with plastic toy soldiers.

In school, those many years ago, more-unsavory kids used them for other purposes. I can remember how—in the hands of skilled delinquents—and optimally stretched—those same rubber bands served as a low-tech counterpart of what the Pentagon black budget crowd now refers to as "directed-energy weapons." With a fair degree of accuracy, those rubber bands delivered painful cranial hits on kids who were hunched over their books... or sneaky posterior strikes on kids who bent over to grab something they'd dropped.

Here's something else I remember: If the shooter wasn't careful—meaning the rubber band slipped off their finger during the crucial pre-fire stretch—the snapback effect turned the perpetrator into the victim.

The same thing happens in the financial markets when over-exuberant investors stretch a stock too far—to the upside or downside—and feel the sting from an unplanned snapback.

Identify the snapback *before* it happens, however, and you can ride the Rubber Band—and avoid its sting.

Now that our screening process has culled the universe of stocks down to a manageable basket of potential winners, we'll zero in on the ones that have been stretched to their physical limits (meaning they're now extreme stocks). These are otherwise healthy stocks that are extremely oversold (don't worry, I'll fully explain that in just a minute). But that's a temporary condition. Indeed, their longer-term outlook is actually quite bullish.

Specifically, we're talking here about stocks that are:

- Actually in a long-term uptrend.
- But have become *temporarily* oversold.

We're going to use two elementary tools to help us identify these stocks. They are:

1. Simple Moving Averages (SMAs), which can spotlight those otherwise healthy stocks that are in long-term uptrends.
2. And the Relative Strength Index (RSI), which can pinpoint stocks that are extremely oversold (stretched to their limits).

Once you've done this, you'll have targeted a handful of stocks whose prices are currently depressed ... but that are also very likely to snap back—for *huge* short-term profits.

The bottom line ...

You are now ready to Frame the Trade.

The Trend Is Your Friend

It was August 1940, and Prime Minister Winston Churchill was visiting a Royal Air Force (RAF) fighter squadron that was feeling the brunt of the daily Luftwaffe attacks during the pivotal Battle of Britain. As the story goes, Churchill told his chief military assistant—Major General Hastings "Pug" Ismay—"Don't speak to me ... I have never been so moved." After a few minutes of quiet contemplation, Churchill then told his friend that "never in the history of mankind has so much been owed by so many to so few."

That sentence formed the basis of a speech Churchill would make to the House of Commons a few days later—a speech that remains one of the most-remembered in history.

The "so few" that Churchill was referring to were the outnumbered fighter pilots of the RAF—a truly amazing group that included fliers like Douglas Bader, an ace who would amass 22 kills, despite flying with two artificial legs.

What the Luftwaffe didn't know . . . couldn't know . . . was that the British had learned a few things from the American militia at Huck's Defeat more than 150 years before . . . including the importance of getting an Edge over a numerically superior adversary.

You see, the Brits were positioned to benefit from a top-secret technology . . . one that would end up providing a *decisive Edge* in the Battle of Britain.

That technology was called radar.

While it seems utterly routine in today's world of GPS and real-time satellite imagery, in the early 1940s, radar ranked somewhere between science fiction and total black magic in terms of its development and potential.

By bouncing radio waves off solid objects—like incoming bombers—and "reading" the returns, British defenders could literally "see" enemy attackers while they were still miles and miles distant . . . even during bad weather . . . and even at night. That meant defending RAF pilots could keep their Hawker Hurricanes and Supermarine Spitfires on the ground until the last possible moment—conserving fuel and maximizing airtime. It also meant the RAF knew where the Luftwaffe attackers were headed. So the British defenders could have their fighter planes hidden in the clouds over the target and be ready to pounce on the enemy attackers when they arrived.

Talk about getting an Edge.

The Colonial Minutemen had set the same kind of trap for the British Redcoats in that dense South Carolina forest a century-and-a-half before.

As we well know, of course, the RAF pilots enjoyed the same decisive results as the American colonists.

Indeed, the Battle of Britain turned into such a Luftwaffe rout that the German pilots actually bought into the propaganda line that a healthy diet of fresh carrots gave British pilots the ability to see in the dark (spoiler alert: they couldn't).

Warriors are a lot like financial markets . . . they adapt to changes or shifts. Soon, the German bomber crews adopted a zigzag strategy in the

English skies to help disguise their intended flight paths—and ultimate targets.

The German High Command's thinking was that—if the Luftwaffe bombers didn't take a direct approach—the beta-carotene-juiced RAF aces would be forced to follow them, would run through their fuel, and would be unable to focus their firepower at the Luftwaffe's most-vulnerable moment ... when the German attackers were over the target and on their final bombing run.

It was now Britain's turn to adapt. Crafty British radar operators developed an exceedingly simple method for accurately forecasting the bombers' intended targets—despite the seemingly random directional changes that were supposed to obfuscate the Germans' *real* objectives. By averaging out the Germans' course adjustments over time, the Brits could filter out the random noise and accurately predict a trend.

So when the Luftwaffe Dornier, Heinkel, and Junkers bombers arrived over their targets, they found squadrons of Spitfires and Hurricanes there and ready to take them out.

If that sounds a lot like forecasting the direction of a whipsaw stock market ... well, you are right on target, too. And that brings us to the directional tool we'll be using in this section—something called the Simple Moving Average (SMA).

At its most basic level, the SMA is nothing more than an average of data points (like closing stock prices) for a set number of previous periods (typically, trading days). Some of the most commonly used time periods are 20, 50, and 200 trading days.

It's a moving average because—as we progress through the calendar—a new price point is added to the average for the current day, while the oldest number in the series falls off.

Here's an example.

Let's say it's April 30, and I'm calculating a 30-day moving average of high temperatures in Fargo, North Dakota. Today, I total up the high temps for all 30 days in that month, and then divide by 30.

Simple enough.

Tomorrow, however, I'll add the temp for May 1 and drop the one from April 1. I still have 30 days' worth of data to average. But I've moved the time span forward one day.

And that's where we get the "moving" component of a "moving average."

As the crafty British radar operators did with the zigzagging Luftwaffe bombers in our story about the Battle of Britain, we're going to use the SMA tool as a smoothing device that filters out the daily price fluctuations so we can more clearly see longer-term trends. By changing the number of days in the average, I can choose to assess trends over shorter—or longer—periods of time. The more days I include, the smoother the average will typically be. (See Figure 5.9.)

For identifying and trading Rubber Bands we'll use the 200-day moving average—a widely used long-term trend indicator.

And we will say that stocks trading above their 200-day moving average are in a "long-term uptrend." I've looked at many different directional filters for this strategy, and this 200-day moving average is consistently the most useful one (in addition to being easy to use and understand).

Figure 5.9   Simple Moving Average (SMA)
SOURCE: Chart courtesy of StockCharts.com

Momentum and the RSI

Now that we've learned to identify stocks in a long-term uptrend, the next step is to find those that are temporarily oversold.

In simple terms, we're looking for stocks that are experiencing a general uptrend—but that have experienced a swift pullback ... for one reason or another.

There are many catalysts, or triggers, for a sell-off of this type.

We could be talking about profit-taking, a large block-order liquidation from an institutional trader, worrisome rumors, or even news that's "external" to the company or stock. Most likely it's pure herd psychology. As we now know from our brief study of auction markets and trader psychology, once a stock starts selling off, other traders (not wanting to be the last one out) follow suit, dumping their shares and driving the price lower.

Instead of joining the herd and following the market lemmings off the cliff, the 10-Minute Millionaire sees these extreme downside blips as buying opportunities. Once traders realize the selling was way overdone—and grasp that the stock is now actually cheap—we expect them to jump back in and bid the stock back up.

But you don't have to rely on expectations or guesses. There's actually a tool that can help you quantify which stocks are oversold—and to what degree.

It's called the RSI.

RSI is an oscillator that fluctuates between zero and 100. And it measures both the speed and magnitude of the price changes. Traditionally, an RSI over 70 indicates an overbought stock. An RSI of less than 30 generally tells us that a stock is oversold.

In simple terms, RSI is a tool that tells us how far and how fast a stock's price has moved. It's part of a family of signals that technical analysts call "momentum indicators." (The engineer in me must confide that these indicators don't really measure momentum in the classical physics definition of the word).

If you just focus on how far the price moved—and how fast it made that move—then you're well on your way to understanding RSI and other similar momentum indicators.

As an interesting aside, this is another indicator introduced by Welles Wilder in his groundbreaking 1978 book *New Concepts in Technical Trading Systems*. For the record, I have no particular affinity for Wilder's indicators in general. But I have to say that he did a great job creating what is now a suite of core trading indicators found in practically every charting package.

If you want to dig into the math, the equation follows here. You don't have to know this calculation to follow the 10-Minute Millionaire system. But I know there are probably two or three of you out there who want to know the calculation.

For those of you in this inquisitive group, here's how software packages calculate RSI:

$$RSI = 100 - 100/(1 + RS)$$

Where,

RS = Average of × Days up closes/Average of × Days down closes.

Thankfully, you don't have to do this math. StockCharts.com (or your trading platform of choice) will do it for you. But we wanted to run through it here because some of you will be interested in the underlying concepts at work.

Just like the SMA, we can measure RSI over any period we like. Since the RSI is measuring the average gain divided by the average loss over the selected time frame, longer time periods lead to a greater smoothing effect. Typically, traders look at the 14-day RSI as a sort of default time frame. But since we're hunting for *extremely* short-term weaknesses in an overall long-term uptrend, we'll select a three-day RSI as our Rubber Band indicator.

And we'll keep this in mind.

Harkening back to our anecdote about the rubber-band-shooting classroom troublemaker... remember what we're really looking to achieve here. We're *not* searching for Rubber Bands that are only nominally stretched, meaning they'll fly a few short feet, and end up on the floor—well short of their intended target.

We're out to find Rubber Bands that are stretched right to their absolute limit ... that have so much stored energy that their release will send them zooming across the classroom ... with an accuracy that lets us pick off the housefly that came to rest on the Red Delicious apple left on the teacher's desk.

Given that objective, the standard-fare RSI—an oversold indicator at 30 or just below—just won't cut it for us.

At *minimum*, I'm looking at RSIs under 10. Below 5.0 is even better—but that comes with a trade-off.

In general, the lower the RSI trigger, the fewer the number of trading opportunities you'll see. But the ones you do find will be the extreme of the extreme—and will tend to experience the biggest snapbacks for the biggest gains when they do.

Option #1	Option #2
RSI < 10	RSI < 5
More trades	Fewer trades
Lower percent return	Higher percent return

Here again, we're talking about an input (a parameter) of the 10-Minute Millionaire system that you can tailor to meet your own goals once you've achieved expert status with this trading strategy. As you use this system more, feel free to tune the approach based on your own trading experience, trading style, and risk tolerance. For now, however, we're sticking with the formula I believe has the best chance of bringing you early and consistent success.

Putting It All Together

Here's where the rubber (band) meets the road.

First, pop up your chart viewer. Make sure you include a 200-day Simple Moving Average (SMA (200)) and your 3-day RSI indicator (RSI(3)) as your default setting.

Second, start paging through the 50 or so stocks that you pre-screened back in Section 1 of this chapter as Fast Movers.

Look for any candidates with an RSI under 10 (or under 5) that are also above the 200-day moving average.

A typical Rubber Band opportunity will look like what's shown in Figure 5.10.

Figure 5.10   Classic Rubber-Band Setup
SOURCE: Chart courtesy of StockCharts.com

Shortcut Tip

If you only want to screen the market for Rubber Band opportunities, you can further simplify your analysis by combining the initial screen for Fast Movers with the Rubber Band criteria. Just add parameters that filter for stocks showing:

- Price > 200-Day Simple Moving Average
- 3 (or 2) Day Relative Strength Index < 10 (or 5)

See Figure 5.11 for what a StockCharts.com scan function would look like.

Where MV is your minimum volatility as discussed earlier, and RS is your relative strength trigger.

Next up, we'll Frame the Trade by putting on risk controls and setting contingency exits (stop-loss orders) to limit your downside on the 35 percent to 45 percent of Rubber Bands that *break* instead of snapping back (depending on market conditions).

```
Scan Criteria:

[type = stock]
and [Country is US]
and [SMA(14, Volume) > 500,000]
and [Close > 5.00]
and [ATR(14) / Close > MV]
and [Close > SMA(200)]
and [RSI(3) < RS]
```

Figure 5.11 Scan Criteria

That's a portion of the strategy that will help you maximize your gains, while minimizing your losses.

In the long run, this reward-to-risk structure is where the real money is made—where wealth is achieved. But you must survive to get there.

So always remember this . . .

It's in the long run where 10-Minute Millionaires are ultimately crowned.

But those millionaires are made piece by piece in the short term . . . when they have learned the system, and avoided the losses that keep them from achieving this exalted status.

We intend to help you get there.

CHAPTER 6

Framing the Trade

W e've all heard those opening lines to the iconic poem about Paul Revere, the silversmith and Revolutionary War Patriot whose midnight gallop warned American colonists that the Redcoats were marching on Concord and Lexington.

And most of us believe we know what U.S. radio commentator Paul Harvey used to refer to as "the rest of the story"—that Longfellow's poem is really wrong, and that riders other than Revere actually did most of the riding and warning.

But here's the *real* "rest of the story"—which is both instructive and pretty cool.

The gist of Longfellow's poem is factually accurate. On the eve of Concord and Lexington—the battles that launched the Revolutionary War—Revere *did* ride out to warn colonists of a pending raid by British forces. The rest of the story is pretty much an embellishment written 80 years later to ignite a surge of patriotic nationalism.

Call it Civil War propaganda.

Interestingly enough, historians today obsess over the poem's inaccuracies—so much so, in fact, that lots of folks regard Longfellow as a sloppy researcher. In reality, just the opposite is true: the poet *thoroughly* researched his subject. The inaccuracies in Longfellow's poem—if you want to call them that—were put there on purpose.

Longfellow had set out to turn Revere into a full-fledged American folk hero—just as he'd done with the Pilgrims' Myles Standish.

So if turning Paul Revere into an American hero . . . a legend . . . was Longfellow's goal, I think we can all agree that he succeeded—mistakes or not.

I've always loved that story—and not just because of my affinity for American history.

I also like it because the *true* story of what happened to Paul Revere on that history-making spring night in April 1775 contains several valuable lessons for traders and investors.

And those lessons are particularly applicable to the 10-Minute Millionaire.

Before we start, however, let's take a few seconds to understand exactly where we are on our own journey of discovery.

When You Fail to Plan . . .

Remember, now, that we were in the hunt for stocks experiencing pricing extremes.

We're talking here about stocks that had been in long-term uptrends. For whatever reason, these stocks were pushed out of that trend. Out of that group, we've zeroed in on the stocks we believe are poised for a snapback—meaning they'll spring back and resume their former long-term uptrend.

That brings us to our next step.

You see, even though we now have a handful of extreme stocks—specifically, those we believe have the highest probability for a snapback—we're not just going to race ahead and start putting on trades.

As is true of every step in this process, we first want to plan our next move.

Specifically, we need a predetermined *exit plan*.

In virtually any potentially high-risk activity you can think of, participants don't move until they have their exit plan in place.

By "exit plan," we're referring to a trading escape route.

A Plan B.

A backup plan.

Call it whatever you wish, but here's the reality: if you know you're involved in a risky situation, it pays to take extra precautions.

Consider these examples.

Firefighters never attack a blaze without knowing their escape route first. And that goes double for the so-called smoke jumpers who parachute into the remote wildlands of the Pacific Northwest to battle the wicked forest fires that we read about every summer.

Skydivers have a backup strategy, too: they use automatic deployment devices to pop their chutes at a preset altitude in case they get distracted or otherwise incapacitated. And they have backup chutes for the rare cases when their main canopy fails to open.

Pilots—private, commercial, and military—identify intermediate airports along their route ... and do so while filing their flight plans ... *before* strapping themselves into the cockpit. And they take these steps "just in case."

I can hear some of you thinking to yourselves—or even responding out loud: "Well, sure, D.R.—but these are all life-and-death initiatives you're talking about here."

That's true. But isn't it true that the stakes are just as high when it comes to your money? Aren't we really trying to mitigate the risk of killing your financial future?

When you consider it from that vantage point, investing is kind of a life or death proposition.

Success as an investor means life—which means success. And not just for you. I'm talking about things like:

- A wonderful retirement, with the money for you and your spouse to travel, to indulge in hobbies and other life passions, and to cover your health needs.

- A fulfilling life for your daughter or son—because you were able to help them attend a really good college.
- A happy, healthy, and safe golden years' story for your folks. They took care of you during your formative years; now you can pay them back by making sure they have good healthcare, a cozy place to live and occasional dinners out, trips to warm-weather spots, and long visits with the grandchildren you've brought into the world for them.
- An ability to give back and help others not as fortunate—perhaps helping fund that local food pantry, aiding programs that rescue kids or pets from horrid domestic circumstances, or assisting your church as it sends inner-city kids to summer camp at a lush riverbank campground.

Conversely, investing failure is followed by death—death of the worldwide travel plans you and your spouse have had for 40 years; death of your dream to send your kid to medical school; the deathlike feelings you experience when there's no money to help your folks in their time of need.

So even as an investor, you really do have *lots* on the line.

And yet . . . during my career as a speaker, investment coach, and seminar leader—where I get to hear so many "if I'd only known" laments—I'm astonished time and again by how few traders take time to craft even the *simplest* escape route precautions when their personal economic livelihood is at risk. They fire off one trade . . . then another . . . then a third—as if it's just one big video game.

But investing isn't a video game. There isn't a reset button. There are no do-overs.

In the financial markets—just as we see with the Northwest smoke jumpers—mistakes are often final and fatal.

Big losses are very difficult to recover from. It doesn't matter if that hefty loss is incurred all at once—after taking a single, too-large position—or if it's more of a "death by a thousand cuts," thanks to a series of smaller, but-still-ill-advised trades.

As I note repeatedly in media interviews, in trade alerts to my newsletter subscribers, and in seminars, if you lose 50 percent of your portfolio because of bad trades, you have to double your remaining capital (earn a 100 percent return)—just to get even.

Even smaller losses leave you with a long, stressful journey back to breakeven. For example, lose 25 percent of your holdings and you have to earn 33 percent just to get back to your starting point.

Those are long odds—especially if your trouble started because of inadequate safety measures.

Without a plan, without preplanned escape routes, without accounting for risk, it's just too easy to lose track of your position and make stupid mistakes.

The 10-Minute Millionaire always has a plan.

Always.

I refer to this phase of our process . . . of our system (managing risk before we pull the trigger) . . . as Framing the Trade.

And it's critical.

If you talk to investing pros, they'll talk about "putting on a trade."

That's Wall Street lexicon for the purchase of a stock, or options contracts, or futures.

But success as a trader is about much more than the positions you take, than the trades you put on.

I'm talking about an actual framework—a structural skeleton that will pull all the pieces of our dynamic trading process together, and hold it together over time.

Our framework provides boundaries. It's an anchor for the stretched and pulled market extremes we target and profit from. It's responsible for the structural rigidity that holds escape routes open—so we can get out in the instances when our trades don't work out.

To give you the rest of the picture, let's go back to the rest of the story. Let me finish the Revolutionary War tale I used to open this chapter.

I'm talking, of course, about Longfellow's poem—*Paul Revere's Ride.*

A Contingency Plan to Revere

It was April 1775, and long-simmering tensions in the American Colonies were fast coming to a boil.

There hadn't been any shooting yet. But the tenor in and around Boston was especially strident.

The British garrison there—led by General Thomas Gage—had been ordered to crack down on the rebellious colonists who were blatantly challenging British rule.

For months, General Gage and his men had been raiding private residences, as they searched for guns and ammunition and arrested Colonial provocateurs. The colonists there were getting pretty fed up with these British aggressions and an organized resistance was taking shape.

One day in April, General Gage learned of a hefty rebel arms cache in Concord, roughly 20 miles northwest of his location. He decided to march 700 of his men—all Redcoat regulars—to that town to seize and destroy the weapons. Success at this, he reasoned, would crush the nascent rebellion in a single, decisive blow.

So he ordered one of his men—Lieutenant Colonel Francis Smith— to move from Boston "with utmost expedition and secrecy to Concord, where you will seize and destroy . . . all military stores."

The extent of his plan seemed to be: "Hey, I've got lots of armed guys. These colonists have been relative pushovers in the past. I'll just go out and end this thing—end it once and for all. Bunch of bloody upstarts. I'll show them who's boss."

Unfortunately, there were contradictions—even inconsistencies— in this plan. While wanting his adjutant to seize the weapons, General Gage also did not specifically order (in written form) the arrest of rebel leaders, fearing this might spark an uprising (as if marching into a rebel stronghold and seizing weapons wouldn't do the exact same thing).

As we'll see, Gage's failure to fully frame his plan—to entertain the possibility of failure, to factor in an escape route, and to add a "what comes next" step to his strategy—would prove disastrous.

In a bit of reality that reminds me so much of the financial markets, Gage *knew* about the colonists' weapons horde. But the colonists *knew* that he knew.

And responded accordingly.

Little did the Brits know that a Patriot spy network—known as the Sons of Liberty—had gotten word weeks before Gage moved out that the Colonial weapons might be at risk. So the Patriots shifted the guns, musket balls, and gunpowder to other locations.

They also received details about the route the British would be traveling on their march toward Concord and Lexington—as well as specifics of the Redcoat attack plan.

With intelligence gold like that in hand, such Patriot leaders as John Hancock and Samuel Adams were able to craft plans for a counterattack.

Back in Boston, Paul Revere and William Dawes, a local tanner, were given a special task—to sound the alarm once the British were moving. This would be no poetic solo ride. In real life, Revere knew that the risk of capture or delay for a single rider was huge. So he did the smartest thing possible.

He created a backup plan.

Rather than stake the fate of a budding nation on one horse and rider (the military equivalent of a "bet the ranch" trade), Revere diversified his risk across multiple "trades." He recruited help from the whole network of supportive colonists—all of whom shared the goal of independence and economic freedom from Europe.

On the night of April 18, 1775, the usually precise Redcoats mustered clumsily along the riverfront and shuffled onto barges for their trip across the Charles River. Revere's compatriots were ready. On the far side of the river, two collaborators named Robert Newman and John Pulling Jr. crept into the Old North Church and quietly climbed its tall steeple. They quickly lit two lanterns and shone them for a mere 60 seconds.

That was all it took.

Minutes later, no fewer than 30 riders (some reports place the number as high as 40) raced across Middlesex County, triggering a flexible—but easy-to-implement—"alarm and muster" warning system that had been designed in detail *months* before. You could almost look at this as if the colonists had diversified their risk by "putting on" a bunch of trades. If one "trade" went bad—if one person were stopped, arrested (or shot)—the other trades would still pay off, meaning the warning would still be disseminated.

An hour later, when Revere began his own fabled ride, the alarm was already being sounded across the land.

He just served as the cleanup hitter.

By the time the British marched off their boats in Cambridge, word had spread to towns as far as to 25 miles away—a truly astonishing achievement in an era long before the introduction of clattering telegraph keys and chuffing railways.

The glow of signal fires, ring of bells, and bleat of trumpets told the Redcoats that they'd lost the all-important element of surprise. Unlike the colonists, the British had put their eggs in one basket, and had put on just a single trade. And this wasn't framed as part of a well-conceived system. The British trade lacked a risk-management component. It lacked an escape route. It lacked a stop-loss point.

Like a trader who refuses to acknowledge an unanticipated stock-market shift, British officers stubbornly stuck to their original plan and stoically pushed on, marching their troops along a soggy route that was now an open secret.

Revere's respect for risk proved prescient, for *he was* captured that night . . . and *before* he reached Concord.

Revere and Dawes were being accompanied by a Dr. Samuel Prescott (who happened to be in Lexington, returning from a lady friend's house at the awkward hour of 1 A.M.).

In a town called Lincoln, the trio ran into a Redcoat roadblock and were detained. Prescott escaped by jumping his horse over a wall. Dawes also got away, though he fell off his horse soon after. He didn't complete his ride and, in fact, had to come back later to find the watch he'd dropped. Revere was held at gunpoint.

It was the Revolutionary War equivalent of a trade gone badly. But thanks to Revere's advance planning, and allowance for risk, that one bad "trade" didn't matter.

Prescott reached Concord. And other riders circulated the warning into the remotest parts of the region.

The system that had been put in place ahead of time continued to operate as its creators intended—even without Revere personally pushing it forward.

Thanks to the well-circulated warning, armed Colonial militia were soon assembling at predetermined choke points along the route the Redcoats were traveling.

When the British reached the town square at Lexington, the militiamen were waiting. A tense standoff began. Would the British, knowing that fierce Colonial resistance awaited them, push on? Or would those Redcoats retreat, shifting their strategy to instead seek a political solution to the colonists' grievances?

The answer was the "shot heard 'round the world"—the beginning of the battles of Concord and Lexington, memorialized in yet another poem—this one called *Concord Hymn,* and penned by Ralph Waldo Emerson.

The Revolutionary War had begun.

But our story isn't over—not just yet.

The militiamen were outnumbered at Lexington and fell back. The British Regulars proceeded to Concord, where they broke into smaller groups in search of the rumored supplies.

For the Redcoats, however, Concord was a trap—again because of a Patriot contingency plan that had been carefully designed ahead of time.

By 11 A.M. on April 19, 1775, a new wave of Patriots had arrived from surrounding farms and villages.

Putting Concord's narrow North Bridge to strategic use, they ambushed the Redcoats. As the luckless British soldiers approached, 400 concealed militiamen engaged 100 Redcoats who were squeezed together in a confined column.

Confused, the British officers attempted a defensive move that had been designed for the narrow streets and alleys of city battles. The colonists fanned out to avoid the Redcoats' focused cone of fire and peppered the enemy from the sides.

The bloodshed was heavy—but only on one side.

It was the British who were beaten back—victimized by their own poor planning. In fact, they fell back with such haste that many of their wounded comrades were actually abandoned along the way. And as the Redcoats retreated to Boston, the colonists' advance planning continued to pay off.

New waves of militiamen streamed in to intercept the British soldiers. These colonists would take positions at strategic points along the path of retreat, would subject the Loyalist troops to withering crossfire—and then would leapfrog to new positions, where they could blast away again.

By the end of the battle—a fight whose ferocity stunned both sides—British casualties outnumbered the Patriots' by a 3 to 1 margin.

The Agony of Defeat

This 240-year-old story isn't precisely analogous to the 10-Minute Millionaire trading approach, but the concepts are remarkably congruent and the lessons certainly poignant.

Perhaps the most dramatic statement I can make here is that—in this tale—the British remind me an awful lot of the hordes of irrational traders that we're aiming to profit against.

Really. Just take a minute to consider what actually happened—including the deadly costs incurred.

In this story, the Redcoats allowed their actions to be guided by a false sense of security—even invincibility. I've seen that very same arrogance in traders—over and over again. And I can typically identify the trading newbies who have a similar (future) date with disaster.

The Redcoats here were so haughty that they couldn't conceive of being beaten by the other players active in the "market"—namely the colonists. Before the Revolution—indeed, for much of the war—British officers viewed the Colonial militiamen with abject contempt. Even the Redcoat soldiers—the British Army regulars—believed their counterparts were low-quality soldiers who represented the absolute dregs of New World society.

In reality, the Americans came from all walks of life, from all levels of society—but they shared a uniform toughness that contributed mightily to colonists' ultimate victory.

Underestimating the risks they faced was just one of the mistakes the British leaders made.

Again, like too many traders I've watched, the British Army came into the war fixated on the big win. Before Concord and Lexington, these Brits wanted to swoop in and capture all the colonists' arms—stopping hostilities before they got started. It was a laudable goal—and clearly a high-return proposition. But it was also high risk. And the Brits launched this high-risk/high-return trade with no risk management, with no escape route, and with no acknowledgment of the possibility that this "trade" could go against them.

They were focused on the upside gain (capturing a huge supply depot) and figured it was an easy hit. They'd had few problems before. But these earlier probes were done on the fringes: they searched some houses, and arrested a handful of rabble-rousers. But these missions were sporadic, and weren't focused on a big cache of arms.

This pre-Concord attitude is a lot like the trader who, after a couple of small—and probably lucky—market wins, decides it's time to go for broke and puts a big slice of his investment capital at risk on an all-or-nothing trade.

And gets his clock cleaned.

As soon as the British saw that the all-important element of surprise was lost, they should have pulled back, regrouped, and conceived a new plan—one using different tactics or with a higher probability of success. That's what a 10-Minute Millionaire would do.

Instead, the Redcoats stayed in their trade—pressing an already bad situation to make it worse. They were emotionally vested. Too much had already gone into the mission to admit defeat. Already at a disadvantage, they doubled down and pushed a bad trade into a total disaster.

Traders make this very same mistake all the time. They've taken a big position—maybe even on margin—and then it goes against them. Instead of closing the trade, taking the loss and moving on, they stick with it—perhaps even propping it up with new capital, even as the position continues to fall in price.

In the markets—and on the battlefield—this is how painful-but-still-manageable losses turn into total wipeouts.

Now let's look at the players on the other side of the battlefield.

Separating Winners from Losers

In this battle at the start of the Revolutionary War, our Redcoat "traders" made just about every mistake possible.

However, on the opposite side of the battlefield, the Minutemen got it right. They unknowingly followed the 10-Minute Millionaire playbook—almost perfectly.

First, they *identified an extreme.*

The colonist soldiers understood that the British Army was really an aggregation of many, many irrational individuals—not unlike the financial markets of today.

They had a belief that General Gage and his officers would be driven by their egos and overconfidence to pursue an ill-advised, or ill-conceived, strategy.

Rather than randomly and recklessly risking scarce assets on an imperfect situation, the Patriots conducted relentless "market research" (spying) to identify an extreme opportunity in which the probabilities were greatly in their favor.

The Sons of Liberty were their screening tool. The spies' intelligence network screened for the perfect slice of the market (Concord), identified a long-term uptrend (the fight for freedom), and waited for things to get out of whack—which is precisely what happened as the Redcoats pushed their ill-advised strategy.

Having done that spadework, the colonists *went ahead and framed their trade.*

They put planned *contingency stops* in place—like the multiple riders sounding the alarm across the entire countryside and the "staggered entries" with fresh troops being placed at an array of locations both in and around Concord and on the Redcoats' retreat route back to Boston.

To protect the bulk of their assets from being blown up if things went *really* wrong, they moved most of their munitions out of harm's way in a classic example of "position sizing."

They then "*put on the trade*" (launched their strike) in earnest when the Redcoats were pulled into a dense mass at their most vulnerable extreme—at the narrow bridge.

Finally, the militiamen *booked their "profits"* using "moving stops" on the British retreat back to Boston (a concept we'll address in the next chapter).

In short, the Patriots "framed" (planned) the entire encounter from start to finish, leaving no room for chance.

As a teaching opportunity—what folks referred to as a case study back during my days in business school when I was studying for my MBA—this is a rich and instructive story.

And it's a tale I believe has you well-positioned to see and understand these concepts put to use in the stock market.

So let's put that newfound knowledge to work . . .

I Wanna Hold Your Hand

In this section, I'm going to teach you exactly how to *frame each trade* for maximum Edge by taking three steps.

To do that, you will:

1. *Set your Contingency Exit*—Since, generally speaking, one out of every three trades is likely to go against us, we approach each trade

with the worst-case scenario in mind. Before even putting on a position, we first ask ourselves a single question: "How do I get out of this trade if it goes against me?" The most successful traders ask this same question—before each and every trade they are considering. We'll address that question by setting contingency exits in the form of stop-losses. I'll show you how to do that—for proper protection. There's a science to setting these trigger points. You want to set these contingency exits far enough from your entry point to keep from getting stopped out as a result of normal volatility. But you want them close enough to protect your downside should the Rubber Band break instead of snapping back and catapulting you to big gains.

2. *Size the Position*—This may be the single-most-important piece of your risk-management strategy. And with good reason: it's the one variable that separates the trading version of one-hit wonders like Lipps Inc. ("Funkytown"), The Vapors ("Turning Japanese") or Men Without Hats ("Safety Dance") from hit-machine legends like The Beatles or U2. As we've discussed before, it's a quantitative approach that excises emotions or flawed thinking. In a step-by-step tutorial, I'll walk you through the calculation that yields the optimal dollar amount for each position. By doing this, each trade will be sized in a manner that allows you to reap the peak gains of my probabilistic system—while also weathering the occasional (and inevitable) losers.

3. *Put on the Trade*—Finally, we'll show you how to create the trade at the right moment for maximum effect. At this same juncture, we'll also preset our risk controls so that—no matter how the trade plays out—we'll be protected. We'll be able to go about our daily schedule—working, cooking, taking our kids to school or to baseball practice, going to the movies, meeting family members for dinner. And we'll be able to do this knowing that our "trusted employee"—our system—is minding the store. That, after all, is the mission (or value proposition) of the 10-Minute Millionaire system. With this system up and running in the background, we can go about our business. But we can drop in, see what the stock screen has uncovered, and position new trades. Once you have your system operating, you really can maintain it with investments of as little as 10 minutes at a time.

With the benefit of this overview, let's move on to examine the frameworks of trades in much deeper detail.

And we'll start with downside protection—in essence, an automated trigger that gets us out of a bad trade before it becomes a disastrous one.

Downside Protection

As we've explained, contingency exits in the form of stop-orders are a critical part of the 10-Minute Millionaire system. These stop-orders act like a safety net. Once in place, our stops just sit there—below our entry price—waiting to catch us if we stumble on a particular trade.

If the stock we're trading breaks down—for whatever reason—and hits our stop, it triggers an automated sell order at the market price. That gets us out—free and clear of the trade. And because of our system's role as our trusted employee—the trusted staffer who looks out for our interests—this happens whether we're at our desk watching the trade on our computer monitor . . . or at work . . . or out on the links, enjoying a round of golf.

It's reassuring to have this safety factor in place.

Really reassuring.

Let's look at how we do it.

And we'll begin by noting that there's no way to create a *perfect* stop (at least not consistently on every trade, time and time again).

But that doesn't mean we can't put on *really good* stops that, over the long haul, give us a high degree of downside protection. We can employ some pretty simple math to:

- Give ourselves a bit of leeway for the stock to fluctuate before hitting our stop-loss.
- And do so while still keeping that trigger point close enough to the entry price to limit the losses on the trades that do go south.

So how do we get to this right price for our stop?

Would something as simple as a fixed dollar amount—say, a drop of $2 a share on all stocks—do the trick?

Nope. Unfortunately, stocks don't all trade at the same price level. So we'll get wide variations in our risk controls.

Let me show you what I mean.

On a $40 stock, a two-point ($2-a-share) loss represents a 5 percent hit.

But on a $7 stock, that same two-buck hit represents a painful loss of nearly 30 percent.

Clearly, we need something more precise and consistent.

How about a fixed percentage instead? That way, regardless of the share price of the stock we're trading, the percentage loss will be the same across all trades. It's a good idea, and a step in the right direction.

The problem, unfortunately, is volatility.

It's actually a bit of a paradox.

I mean, we *like* trading volatile stocks. That price action is our friend. Without it—without a shifting of share prices—there is no profit.

Again, however, there are issues: volatility isn't the same across all stocks at all times.

Remember our minimum volatility screen back in Chapter 5, Part I when we screened for Fast Movers? It's just a minimum. We're always going to shoot for the more volatile stocks with the highest potential for fast gains. By definition, that means these stocks jump around . . . a lot.

By using a fixed percentage for our stop, we risk getting stopped out of most of our most volatile trades during normal trading action. Then again, if we set our stops too loose, we risk big losses.

We could turn to trading charts, to a discipline known as technical analysis.

Maybe you've heard about support and resistance?

You can actually see this on the charts used by technical analysts, a group known as "chartists" for their reliance on these depictions.

In each case, we're talking about price levels at which a critical mass of traders have an irrational bias.

One way to think of a support line or support level is the price at which big groups of technical traders view a stock as a bargain.

Think about door-buster deals we see during the holiday shopping season, and especially on Black Friday. Thanks to seemingly crazy prices retailers offer on laptop computers or flat-panel TVs, folks will line up around the parking lot. It might be a low-quality model of a noted brand name. And it could have been on sale for even less a few weeks earlier.

But whether it really is a bargain—really is a true value—really doesn't matter.

If enough people *think* it's a steal, they will just keep buying. And it won't be long before the shelves will be bare—thanks to a swirl of irrational shopping chaos.

If you understand that mindset, you'll understand that identifying support lines can be a great way to set stops. The theory is that they provide a psychological floor for the share price. Once a stock drops through that support level, the implication is that the buyers are all gone and the stock is likely fall further. Placing a stop at the support point can isolate random trading noise from a true downside break.

Here, too, unfortunately is a problem.

And this problem has to do with the nature of technical chart reading.

By identifying certain trading patterns in stock prices, chartists believe they can understand the thoughts, emotions, and intent of the majority of traders out in the marketplace.

The trouble is, chart reading takes time to master. Like any complex subject, "time at task" is needed. While the ability to read support and resistance levels can be learned, it's clearly a long-term goal.

Until you've developed those skills, we have a more objective approach.

Our 10-Minute Millionaire solution to the age-old, stop-level conundrum can be found in our old friend: Average True Range (ATR).

If you recall, ATR is a measure of short-term volatility. With it, we can measure the true trading range of any stock over any period of time.

Because of this capability, we can ask ATR to do double duty for us. Not only can it help identify the most volatile stocks poised for a fast move, it can also serve as a yardstick to help us place our trading stops.

When our target stock is extremely volatile, the ATR will be higher. So an ATR-based stop will give us more downside leeway while we wait for a volatile stock to snap back. Lower volatility means a smaller ATR—and hence a higher floor. ATR becomes a self-adjusting risk limiter that varies with a stock's volatility—just how we need it to.

Using ATR as our baseline, it's up to us to determine the precise level at or beyond 1 × ATR to place our stop loss. As you might expect, the decision comes with some trade-offs.

A tighter stop will give you lower losses but fewer wins. In other words, you'll get stopped out more often, but when you do, the losses will be minimal.

A loose stop will give your stock more room to fluctuate. You'll get stopped out less often, but when you do, the loss will be greater. On the other hand, that extra wiggle room means more of your trades will be winners.

More precisely, 1.0 times ATR is considered a tight stop while 3.0 times is just too loose to be meaningful.

Beginner	Intermediate	Advanced
1.0 × ATR	1.5 × ATR	2.0 × ATR
Tight	Medium	Loose
Lower average loss	Good compromise	Higher win rate

A stop at 1.0 × is a great place to start when you're first learning the system. It'll serve to minimize your potential loss on each trade while still giving you unlimited upside profit potential. The trades that do get stopped out won't hurt too much as you gain confidence in the 10-Minute Millionaire system. For all of these reasons, you'll enter a sell stop at 1.0 × ATR below the low of the *last three trading days*.

That "last three" metric is key. Most of the time, especially for our extremely oversold candidates, the three-day low is actually the low for the current day.

However, we don't always hit the exact bottom of an oversold opportunity. And that's okay. If there was a lower-low any time in the last three days, that's our benchmark.

The math is pretty simple. Find the current ATR for the stock you're analyzing, subtract it from the lowest low of the last three days, and *voila:* That's your sell-stop price.

Figure 6.1 Proper Stop-Loss Placement
SOURCE: Chart courtesy of StockCharts.com

Following is an example involving Electronic Arts Inc. (Nasdaq: EA). To see how this looks graphically, check out Figure 6.1.

Our trading worksheet makes the process a snap. Just record the relevant metrics and do the simple math:

A. Set Your Contingency Exit

Symbol	Price	200-Day SMA	RSI	3-Day Low	14-Day ATR	Stop (Low − 1 x ATR)	Max Loss (Price − Stop)
EA	$65.53	$57.91	4.29	$64.01	$1.95	$62.06	

I'm first identifying the three-day low, which in this case for EA is $64.01. Then I'm subtracting 1.0 times the ATR, or $1.95 from the three-day low to arrive at my stop loss price. For EA, that means $64.01 − $1.95 = $62.06.

Again, this number is *not* up for negotiation, fudging, rounding, or second-guessing. This is your safety net that ensures positive Edge on the trade by controlling your downside risk.

Now that we've defined our maximum loss on the trade and determined our stop levels, it's time to move on to the next part of our risk-management strategy—the part that I believe to be the most important of all.

I'm talking about position sizing.

Sizing Up the Opportunity

Rookie traders—and some experienced ones—think of stop-losses as a way to limit their overall market risk.

For example, let's say that I'm one of these rookies and that I'm only willing to risk 10 percent of my portfolio on any given trade. So I'll just set my stop 10 percent below each purchase price and call it a day.

This is the wrong approach.

Contingency exits in the form of stop-losses are an integral part of the 10-Minute Millionaire's risk-management process.

But there's a second piece—just as important.

I'm talking about position sizing.

Here's how they fit together:

- Contingency Exits are the parts of our system that tell us how far— the amount we'll allow the price of a share of stock (or options contract, and so on) to move against us before we exit a trade. This limits our downside risk per share on any one trade—to ensure we have a positive Edge. Counterintuitively, stop-losses are determined by our system, not our personal risk tolerance. However, that risk tolerance does factor into the size of the positions we choose to trade, as you'll see next.

- Position Sizing is the part of system that tells us how many—how many shares of stock (or options contracts, and so on) to trade. This controls our overall risk to ensure we have enough capital to trade high-expectancy trades over and over again—even taking us through the inevitable losing streak. Position size is determined by the amount of our trading capital and our risk tolerance.

Let's return to the Electronic Arts example we started building just a few pages ago.

A look at our trading worksheet shows that we have all the inputs needed to nail down the proper position size.

The only subjective variable is our personal risk tolerance on each trade.

As we covered earlier in the position-sizing section, when you're starting out, it's best to just trade the minimum allowable unit (that is, one share or one option contract). Once you've traded the system for a while, it'll become more routine and you can move on to the more robust position sizing calculations I'll describe here.

For our EA example, let's say I'm willing to risk $250 on the trade. This could be 1.0 percent on a $25,000 account, or 2.0 percent on a $12,500 account. All that matters is that you've calibrated your own risk tolerance and are sticking to it. Many pros consider 2 percent a maximum number to risk of your core portfolio to risk on any single trade. If you're taking a small underperforming part of your portfolio to use in the 10-Minute Millionaire system, then you may be comfortable with a slightly higher number in such a very speculative account.

Next, just take your dollars at risk ($250) and divide that by the maximum loss per share as determined by your ATR-based contingency exit ($3.47). The result is your positon size in units (that is, 72 shares).

A. Set Your Contingency Exit

Symbol	Price	200-Day SMA	RSI	3-Day Low	14-Day ATR	Stop (Low − 1 x ATR)	Max Loss (Price − Stop)
EA	$65.53	$57.91	4.29	$64.01	$1.95	$62.06	$3.47

B. Size the Position $250.00 / $3.47 = 72

    Dollars to Risk   Max Loss   # of Shares

Now, let's check the math.

If I buy 72 shares at the current price of $65.53, the total cost (not including commissions) is $4,718.16. My stop is at $62.06. So if EA tanks—and I get stopped out—my net loss will be the $4,718.16 purchase cost minus the $4,468.32 sale proceeds (72 shares × $62.06) or $249.84. That's almost exactly my predetermined $250 dollars at risk on this one particular trade (with a 16-cent fudge factor due to rounding).

All right, we're almost there. Our blueprint for the framework of our trade is almost complete.

We've successfully determined our contingency exits and sized our position.

Now it's time to break out the hammer and nails—and actually build our frame and enter the trade.

Ready to Roll

Up until now, the action has been fast and engaging. We've learned to screen stocks for Fast Movers, identified trigger points for actionable trades, and drew up a structured plan with contingency exits and risk controls. You might think the act of actually putting on the planned trade would be equally intense.

And you'd be wrong.

Conventional wisdom says the thrill of trading is something akin to a 1980s-era bullpen or 1990s boiler room. It's full of frenetic energy and highly caffeinated Wall Streeters juggling phones and barking orders over the din of market action.

The 10-Minute Millionaire's world is far different. He or she gets his or her thrills by successfully running a profit-generating system, not by shooting off rapid-fire trades like an old-school video gamer shooting down Space Invaders or digital Centipedes.

Most of the hard (and exciting) work has been done. The rest is pretty routine and anticlimactic.

But it's still very, very important.

If you are confident, I mean absolutely confident, that you literally have run the preceding parts of the 10-Minute Millionaire process by the book, you're now ready to put hand-on-mouse and enter the trade with real money at risk.

But first, like the good pilots we described in an earlier chapter, let's do a preflight check (you can use your completed trading worksheet as a guide).

Did you Find the Extreme by identifying a target stock that's:

- Showing recent volatility at least twice the broader market?
- Trading above its 200-day moving average?
- With a three-day (or two-day) RSI lower than 10 (or even 5.0)?

Did you successfully frame your trade by:

- Identifying your contingency exit based on ATR?
- Calculating your maximum downside based on the stop-loss price?
- Determining your optimal position size in shares based on your risk tolerance?

If you can say "Yes" to all of these questions (and assuming conditions haven't changed drastically in the few minutes it took you to work through the preceding steps), then it's time to enter the trade.

For our bread-and-butter Rubber Band trade as described before, the entry is a simple market order.

It sounds boring, and it is.

Until you book your first profit, that is. And second. And third ...

Entering a buy order at the market just means you'll execute your full trade at whatever the best prevailing price happens to be at the very split second you place the order. It's the surest, fastest, and simplest way to put on your position. And sure, fast, and simple are each hallmarks of a 10-Minute Millionaire.

Some of you may agonize over the market order. After all, a limit order placed just under the market might gain you a few extra pips on your trade—maybe even enough to cover your commissions.

It's true. Some traders like to milk every last penny out of a trade. Some traders also like to hang around their trade station all day, tweaking their limit orders hoping they'll get hit.

Limit orders also have a downside. While waiting for normal market movement to give you a better entry price, you could miss out on hefty upside opportunities—all because you were trying to chisel out a few extra pennies on your entry.

But the 10-Minute Millionaire way is much simpler—and more time efficient.

The 10-Minute Millionaire trade entry happens like this: when trade conditions are right, when you've successfully identified an extremely oversold stock poised for a snapback, when you've framed your trade properly, you *will* enter a market order at your calculated position size. Most folks will do this after the market closes or before it opens the next morning. Your entry order can then be a market order at, or near, the market open.

No muss, no fuss.

In fact, lots of trades with the 10-Minute Millionaire system have a classic rebound that starts in the morning and pushes up strongly that first day. Entering at or near the market's open allows us to participate in the bounce. Plus, market orders usually receive fair entries on more liquid stocks like the ones we'll trade here, especially at a busy time like the open.

Market Order

The NYSE defines a market order as "an unpriced order to buy or sell a stated amount of a security that is to be traded at the best price obtainable."

Market orders can also be entered before or after market hours, in which case it's known as a "market at open" order.

That's it . . .

Almost.

As the late, great pitchman Billy Mays used to say, "But wait, there's more."

As soon as that market order executes—and I mean as soon as you can possibly click on your Enter key—you will place your sell-stop order at the predetermined price calculated on your trading worksheet. There's no waiting around here.

The buy and stop orders are a package deal. You don't enter the market without both in hand any more than you'd leave your house without your keys or drive your car without a seatbelt.

Lean back . . . relax a second . . . and take a deep breath.

Then reengage.

Record your trade on Step 2C of the trading worksheet located in the Appendix. Then walk away. Go to work. Play with your kids. Hit the gym. Live your life.

Trades like this can take several days—and as much as several weeks—to play out, so there's no need to monitor the market. Your safety stop is in place, so any additional attention you place on the market is not only a waste of time, it's a siren song that can tempt your irrational impulses.

Instead, forget about it. It's good discipline. Come back the next day for a check-in. If all goes well, in a few days or so it'll be time to close out the trade and book your profit.

I'll show you how in the next chapter.

CHAPTER 7

Book the Profits

All the things I learned from running apply to any survival situation. You learn to be 100 percent obedient to discipline.
—Louis Zamperini, runner, World War II veteran, and protagonist . of the movie and *New York Times* best seller *Unbroken*

Take a deep breath and relax.
You've done some super work to get yourself to this point.
You're now in the trade, properly framed.
And you got there by working the 10-Minute Millionaire system.
You've found an extremely oversold trading opportunity, planned your contingency exit, sized the position, and put on the trade.
You're now poised to realize optimum Edge on a stock that has a high probability of snapping back for a big gain.
But you're also protected by stops that were put in place to hold any unexpected losses to an acceptable level.
Like the long-distance runner striding around that final turn, the bulk of the race is successfully behind you.

To collect your prize, however, you still need to make it across the finish line.

And that means you absolutely can't let up.

At this point, one of three things has happened. I'll call these "Trade Conditions 1, 2, and 3."

It's important to understand each of them. But only Number 3 requires action on your part.

So here they are:

- **Trade Condition Number 1:** You got stopped out. You found an oversold stock—one that had fallen—but it kept on falling after you put on your trade. So it hit your safety net. Your preplaced stop-loss automatically triggered a sell order. And you're out of the trade— free and clear. It's a loss. But it's no big deal. We planned all along for this contingency. Proper position sizing ensured that this one loss (or even a streak of losses) will not devastate your trading account. You have plenty of dry powder in reserve. Just like the Minutemen at Lexington who fell back to Concord to regroup, it's time to fall back and try again under more favorable conditions.
- **Trade Condition Number 2:** The trade has done nothing much at all. Maybe it's up a little. Maybe it sold off a bit—but not enough to trigger your stop. Maybe it's just treading water. Newer traders tend to get impatient or scared at this point. Emotion trumps common sense and these investors start making stupid decisions—and equally stupid moves. All too often, traders in this spot sell the position for a small loss or minuscule gain. And they never allow the full potential of their system to play out—that is, they never realize their maximum Edge. This is a mistake. If you're in Condition Number 2, stay put. Stand pat. Do nothing.
- **Trade Condition Number 3:** Your trade has snapped back as expected. It's up. Maybe even way up. You're in the money. But how and when do you cash in? How do you turn the gains you have on paper into real green . . . into real profits? Do you cut the run short to lock in your gain? Let it ride and get greedy? These are the very questions that befuddle amateur traders who enter the markets without a robust system in place.

The 10-Minute Millionaire always has a plan.

Even here.

In this chapter, I'm going to teach you when to book profits—and show you how to do it when that time comes.

To do this, I want to share another story—this one a tale from my personal past.

It's a great stage-setter.

Catching Your Fair Share

My dad, who has a degree in building construction, a hybrid between architecture and civil engineering, has been my role model for my whole life. Among his many skills, he's an *accomplished* trout fisherman. I grew up in Radford, Virginia, meaning some of the very best trout streams in the country were just over the next pass of the Blue Ridge Mountains. After I learned some of the basics of casting and bait selection, Dad took me along on one of his weekend outings.

My dad is a very special guy. Even though I'm now an adult and a father with children of my own, my dad is someone I continue to respect and admire. He was the best man at my wedding and I turn to him constantly for wisdom and advice and to be the type of servant-leader that I strive to be.

So it's no surprise that—back in my youth—I always sought to impress and please him.

As a young buck, eager to land a whopping rainbow trout, I bounded all over the stream . . . trying different baits and different locations. After a few casts, I'd get impatient. Standing in one spot, I'd see one of my targets break the stream's surface in a nearby pool, or at the widening of the stream (a bit of fish behavior referred to as a "rise"—which occurs while the trout are surface feeding).

I saw other fishermen reeling in their prizes and soon felt impatient and envious.

To outsmart the fish, I switched tactics—and kept shifting to the latest fish sighting.

My dad, by contrast, stayed put. He narrowly defined his approach. He picked the correct bait for the season. And he cast (quite expertly, I must say) into a proven territory. He didn't get distracted by his environment—including big catches by the fishermen downstream.

His patience was rewarded—greatly rewarded, in fact: he ended the day with a modest catch of sizable trout.

I got skunked.

On the drive home—still stinging from my rookie shutout—I asked Dad how he felt catching only a few fish . . . when I'd seen some other anglers pull in some hefty hauls.

Many years have passed since that day, but Dad's response has stayed with me.

"I caught my fair share," he told me.

I've thought about this many, many times since then.

And one thing I realized was the fact that rookie traders make the same kinds of mistakes that I made on the river that day.

They're so hungry for a win (results-oriented bias), so emotionally vested in the need to be right and afraid of getting skunked (loss aversion bias), that they forget the fundamentals of successful fishing. This irrational behavior ends up costing them dearly.

Emotion—impatience—is obviously a big culprit. Rookie traders in Trade Condition Number 2 bring the same impetuous approach to the markets that I brought to fishing. They jump from one trade to the next—thirsting for immediate gratification. When one trade doesn't instantly snap back for a huge profit, they sell and move to where they think the action is downstream. This grass-is-always-greener approach to investing leads to a lot of missed opportunities—and very often leads to big losses.

Akin to impatience, rookies also make the mistake of taking emotional orders from our old nemesis—loss aversion bias. When a stock is up and showing a modest gain, it's extremely tempting—even hardwired into our psyche—to lock in that small profit by selling now. In doing so, traders forego any potential for a true windfall return.

Finally, traders who lack a system are highly susceptible to greed. They have a big profit on the line, but hold on to the stock, wanting even more—even when there are signs the rally is running out of steam (meaning the fish may slip their hook).

Sometimes this works out and the trade does move higher. But then what? How high is high enough?

Once a trader abandons the discipline of a system and decides to trade by gut instinct, a trade can go bad real fast. Without a reliable yardstick to guide their profit-taking decisions, rookies tend to hang on too long. They miss their exit signal and end up surrendering their hard-won profits when a pullback follows.

The 10-Minute Millionaire system is specifically designed to keep us from continually jumping after the next hot stock—and all the hot ones that follow. (That's the fishing sin I committed by constantly moving to the latest fish sighting.)

Similarly, the 10-Minute Millionaire doesn't try to wring every penny out of each and every trade.

The 10-Minute Millionaire aims to book profits by capturing 70 percent, 80 percent, or 90 percent of a big move. Only then, when the trade has played out—through either a Condition Number 1 stop-out or a Condition Number 3 profit—do we move on to the next opportunity.

The 10-Minute Millionaire system is a complete package. It eliminates the emotional biases that lead to wealth destruction. And it keeps you on the right path to profits.

To that end, there are two tools we can put to use to successfully book profits on Condition Number 3 trades. These are:

1. *The Sell Signal:* The Relative Strength Indicator (RSI) we used to identify our extremely oversold stock is also a reliable trigger that indicates when the bulk of a big upside move is finally playing out.
2. *The Trailing Stop:* For stocks that are up substantially—but that haven't yet triggered a full sell signal, we can use our stop-loss in a very special way. It lets us stay in the trade while it continues to go up, meaning we keep profiting as the stock keeps gaining. But if we use it as a *trailing stop*—meaning the stop price slides higher as our stock price moves up—it guarantees we will keep a slice of our profits if that stock reverses course and starts to fall.

Sell Signal

You may recall that the Relative Strength Indicator (RSI) is an oscillator. That is, it fluctuates within a range of zero (extremely oversold) to 100 (extremely overbought). Just as it signaled our entry point on a stock extremely stretched to the downside, it can also serve as a primary indicator to tell us when the resultant snapback has largely run its course.

As stock market investors—because we're human—we are prone to overreaction. That's why stocks and markets experience the extremes that the 10-Minute Millionaire system is designed to exploit. We bid stocks up way past their true value, creating speculative manias or bubbles that are prone to collapse (like the dot-com bubble of 1999–2000).

And investors overreact to the downside, too, punishing stocks in a way that plunges them well below their actual worth.

The aim of the 10-Minute Millionaire is to play on these inflection points and profit from the irrational herd.

In general, we want to see a three-day RSI above 80 (or even 90) as a reliable signal that our stock's snapback has used up its elastic power and is now in an overbought condition—and is possibly ready to settle into a more sedate trading pattern. So, which is it? Is it 80? Or is it 90? Just like our RSI buying trigger, the choice has trade-offs.

An RSI of 80 is a good starting point for beginners learning the 10-Minute Millionaire system. You'll capture most of the gains and insulate yourself from the very real risk of a pullback. Sure, the stock could go higher (indeed, is likely to do so) before the move is played out. But it's important to remember that we're not looking to milk every penny out of each and every trade—since there's added risk associated with such a mindset.

Our goal—like my dad said—is to get our fair share. And to get that fair share—is to do those profitable trades—over and over again based on time-tested metrics.

Once you have some experience under your belt, you can set a higher RSI sell trigger—possibly even coupled with a trailing stop, which we'll discuss next.

Until then, hard-wire in this rule: "At an RSI above 80, sell at the market."

You can do this at any time you find your trade hitting an RSI above 80. Or if you're checking after the markets close or before the markets open, just enter your order to sell at the open.

An example of how it looks is shown in Figure 7.1.

Don't mess around with a limit order for this type of exit just to grind an additional penny or two from the trade: book your profits, get out, and move on to the next trade.

Figure 7.1   Sell Signal
SOURCE: Chart courtesy of StockCharts.com

Trailing Stops

By now, we're all comfortable with the idea of a stop-loss. We've studied them and used them as the central component of our risk-control strategy. Now we're going to put a slight twist on our dependable stop-loss order and ask it to do double-duty as a profit-taking tool.

To this point, we've presented the profit-taking decision as binary. Zero or one. Black or white.

Either sell at the signal, or stand pat and do nothing.

As I said, that's what we've been talking about to this point.

So let's now look at a strategy in between those two.

Right in the middle.

In my seminars and coaching sessions, I sometimes refer to this as my "profit-maximizing secret weapon."

And here it is.

If your stock is up—and I mean by a meaningful amount (2.0 × to 3.0 × ATR, not just one that's trending)—but the RSI hasn't yet broached 80 to signal a sell, there's a hybrid strategy.

And this hybrid approach does three things for us. It:

1. Locks in a guaranteed profit.
2. Preserves your upside should the stock continue to move.
3. And reframes the trade in a way that continues to remove emotion from your trading process.

This secret profit maximizer is a device known as a "trailing stop."

And for something so powerful, the description seems rather mundane.

The trailing stop lets you boost your safety net up a notch as your trade rockets higher.

It creates successively higher floors under your stock—floors that are above your entry point . . . and not below.

See Figure 7.2 for what a trailing stop looks like.

Going back to our earlier example (from Chapter 6) of high-tech gamer Electronic Arts Inc. (Nasdaq: EA), I've ratcheted up my stop level—from 1.0 × ATR below the previous three-day low when I put on the trade (that is, $58 a share) to $62.53. That's $2.28 a share above my entry price of $60.25.

Stop "Trials"
Stock Price

Stop #2
= $62.53

Stop #1
= $58.00

Figure 7.2 Trailing Stop
Source: Chart courtesy of StockCharts.com

With the trade now successfully reframed, my profit envelope is all but guaranteed. Even if EA ends up slumping and the Rubber Band breaks, I've locked in my maximum downside risk. (Truthfully, this technique actually neutralizes the whole concept of "downside.") If the stock trades down and sells at my stop price, my *worst-case scenario* is now a gain of $2.28 per share—or around 4 percent on the trade.

But if the stock continues its snapback run in the days to come, that's *absolutely great:* I'm still 100 percent long the position and can fully capitalize on any additional upside.

Talk about the best of all worlds.

Now on to the nitty-gritty details.

How do we know exactly where to place our trailing stop? The stock is up, so does it matter? Can we just eyeball it and call it a day?

Well, you *could.* By now you should know what I'm about to say next. That's not the 10-Minute Millionaire way.

For trailing stops, we'll return to our old buddy the Average True Range (ATR). Because it's a self-adjusting measure of volatility, we can use it to set the right level for a trailing stop—just like we did for our contingency exit.

In general, 1.5 × ATR below the current low is a good place to start. We should be in the money by now, so it makes sense to give the stock a little more leeway to fluctuate as our predicted snapback plays out.

In the future, you can experiment with different trailing parameters. A trailing stop at 1.0 × ATR should be your bare minimum. A trailing stop at 3.0 × ATR is too loose. Set your trailing stop somewhere between, but remember the trade-offs.

- A tighter stop (for example, 1.0 × ATR) protects more of your profits but lowers your average dollar win per trade. The reason is that your trade is more likely to get stopped out during a volatile trading session.
- A looser stop (for example, 2.0 × ATR) is less likely to get hit, but if it does, most—if not all—of your profit in the trade goes with it.

Trailing-Stop Level Trade-offs

1.0 × ATR	1.5 × ATR	2.0 × ATR
Tight	Medium	Loose
Higher win rate	Good compromise	Higher percent returns

A couple of key points to remember:

1. Once set to a higher level, you *never* lower the stop. Period. Trailing stops are a one-way street. Increases are fine; decreases are not.
2. You may find it necessary, or helpful, to trail your stop more than once and that's okay (as long as you obey point Number 1, discussed earlier).
3. *Don't forget to cancel your old stop* at the same time you enter the new one. Almost all trading platforms have a "cancel and replace" option for open orders—that's the function to use here. The last thing you want is to have a forgotten sell order out there on a position you've long since exited. Here's another quick tip: if you ever find that you made an honest mistake on a trade—opened one accidentally with a stop that wasn't canceled or added shares to a position when you tried to exit (or any other mistaken click of the mouse), your next move is clear: fix it immediately. Close the trade, sell the unintended shares, and reverse whatever you did. Don't stop to assess if things could move in your direction. Don't do any analysis. Just reverse the error. I could write a chapter about traders who didn't immediately correct a mistake—and suffered brutally as a result.

Finally, record your results on your trading worksheet.

(You may also use some Excel templates on www.10-minutemillionaire.com, which we set up so that the calculations—and some other descriptive statistics—are automatically done for you. You'll also be able to monitor your performance.)

Step 3: Book the Profit						
Date	Price	RSI	Trailing Stop	Gross Proceeds	Net Gain / (Loss)	% Gain / (Loss)
9/9/15	$68.50	81.51	62.53	$7,639.50	$1,012.00	15.3%

With the artful use of stops, trailing stops, and profit-taking exits, you're predefining the profit-and-loss envelope that removes the single-biggest cause of poor trading performance—your own emotions (namely greed and fear).

Intermission

What You Can Do with What You Have Learned

You've taken your first step into a larger world.

—Obi-Wan Kenobi

You made it.

Congratulations.

You've just read the core foundation of the 10-Minute Millionaire—a fast-track trading system for creating meaningful wealth.

I know it wasn't always an easy go. It may even feel like you just completed the mental equivalent of an Ironman triathlon. I've helped you stretch and contort some neural pathways out of their normal routines of thinking, challenged your brain, and maybe even worked some cranial muscles you never knew you had.

That's a good thing.

Hopefully, I've given you a nice glimpse of the promising world of the 10-Minute Millionaire. It's a world in which time is a precious resource. It's a place where that resource is spent wisely on life-affirming habits, not financial worry and fear. This gift of time can help you make a fortune. And time can help you enjoy that fortune . . . which, after all, is the whole reason for amassing a fortune in the first place.

The best part: once you understand it and have it up and running, the system that I've designed for you can be maintained in as little as 10 minutes a day.

I've challenged long-held views that may seem natural, or even comfortable, but are actually highly destructive to your financial well-being. These innate human biases are out of control in today's global financial markets. If you look, you can see scores of examples every day.

Those biases—and the out-of-whack extremes they create—are trouble for some . . . and opportunities for others. For the investors who fail to understand and respect those biases, the potential for financial destruction is high.

For us, these biases and the ever-present herd mentality combine to create the very market extremes that we will now work to profit from.

To protect against our own irrational tendencies, I've started to rewire your brain to adopt a systematic approach to investing that neutralizes these caustic emotions. And yet, the 10-Minute Millionaire system isn't mindless. It takes brains and judgment to run. But it's also a neutral and reliable support structure that helps you profit from market extremes while staying protected from financial Armageddon.

Tactically, the process is logical, repeatable, and reliable.

You're talking about three basic steps.

First, you'll Find the Extreme. These extremes are represented by highly volatile stocks (Fast Movers) that are in strong, long-term uptrends—but that, for various reasons, have been temporarily pulled and stretched to an extreme oversold situation. The tools you'll use are the Average True Range (ATR), trading volume, Relative Strength Index (RSI), and Simple Moving Averages (SMA). And you employ them in a precise combination to yield the very best opportunities for a profitable snapback.

Next, you'll Frame the Trade to optimize your Edge in the market—meaning a high upside potential with limited downside risk. You'll do that through a combination of contingency exits (stop-loss orders) and proper position sizing. Once all factors are defined and locked down, you'll be ready to put on the trade decisively and with confidence.

Finally, you'll Book the Profit—either through a sell signal or with an automated trailing stop. You'll record and keep each and every trade for further analysis of your performance. Then you'll start the process all over again, like turning a crank on a money machine.

You now have the tools, mindset, and system to be a true 10-Minute Millionaire. If it feels a little bit like you just went through ground school for pilot training, it is. You have all the knowledge and conceptual resources needed to successfully fly a plane. What you're lacking is real-world experience and practice.

Lots and lots of practice.

In our final section, I'll be your co-pilot. I'll walk you through some sample trades—step-by-step—to get you successfully off the ground and landing safely back on the runway. From here it will be up to you.

Start small and go slow at first. You may feel awkward at the start as you adapt to new concepts and mindsets.

Trust the system. It works.

Before long, it'll become second nature and you'll be well on your way to building true wealth in just 10 minutes a day.

Now, let's see how this all plays out in real life by walking through some actual 10-Minute Millionaire trades step-by-step.

SECTION III

Putting It All Together

CHAPTER 8

Your First Step . . . Toward Your First Million

A journey of a thousand miles begins with a single step.
—Chinese philosopher Laozi

I've always liked that ancient Chinese proverb . . . because it's so powerful . . . and so true.

And it applies to finance just as much as it applies to life.

Here's what I mean.

As I was researching this book, a study from the Institute for Policy Studies think tank found that the richest 400 Americans have a combined net worth of $2.34 trillion. That's equal to the net worth of the bottom 61 percent of the U.S. population—or about 194 million folks.

And when you drill down—and consider American investor/consumers on more of an individual level—the picture is even grimmer.

Another piece of research that appeared as I was writing was the Credit Suisse *Global Wealth Report*—that investment bank's yearly peek at the state of worldwide investing, saving, and wealth. And the findings were . . . astonishing.

After stating that a 1 percent slice of the world's population controls 50 percent of its wealth, Credit Suisse also estimated that a quarter of all Americans have a negative net worth—meaning their wealth is less than zero.

Said Credit Suisse: "If you've no debts and have $10 in your pocket you have more wealth than 25 percent of Americans . . . more than 25 percent of Americans have collectively, that is."

If you're in that situation, you don't have to stay there.

You have just as much a right to be wealthy as anyone else.

And the 10-Minute Millionaire system is designed to help you achieve that status—to become wealthy.

You just have to be willing to start.

One reason so many of the Americans referenced in these two studies aren't wealthy is that the hill seems too steep to climb.

Trust me when I say this . . . it's not.

Just as the journey of a thousand miles begins with a *single step,* the journey to wealth—to millionaire's status—begins with a *single trade.*

And once you've made that first trade . . . and the others that follow . . . you'll find that your journey to wealth is much shorter than you expected.

Especially because you're making that trip in 10-minute increments.

You now possess the mindset, the tools, and the system to become a 10-Minute Millionaire. You have all the knowledge and concepts needed to pilot yourself on this journey.

Here in this final chapter, I'll help you take that first step . . . and the other steps, besides—the steps you need to practice the trading techniques we've covered—and to get the real-world experience running the system I designed for you.

To prepare you for this final step, let's walk through some sample trades—underscoring one more time the key points to keep in mind as you start trading.

Start small and go slow—at least at first. You may feel awkward at the start as you adapt to new concepts and mindsets.

Trust the system—it works.

And as you gain confidence and get more comfortable using it, consider taking a small, underperforming part of your portfolio and using the system to help grow your net worth to a million dollars or more—a move I suggested back in the book's prologue . . . and several times since.

Before long, the 10-Minute Millionaire system will become second nature, and you'll be well on your way to building meaningful wealth in just 10 minutes a day.

Sampling the System

I recommend making at least 50 copies of the trade worksheet (in the appendix at the end of this book and online at www.10-minutemillionaire.com) and diligently completing it for *each and every trade*. After you've used up all 50 copies, the 10-Minute Millionaire system should feel like *your* system. From there, you can decide whether to continue using the worksheets. (Worth noting: most of the trading pros I know *still* use some form of trade-tracking and journaling to study their wins and losses and to refine their technique).

The trading worksheets will serve a similar purpose here, giving you a perfect record of your trading results to analyze and study as you continue to refine this powerful system and make it your own.

By way of recap, the 10-Minute Millionaire uses the following workflow steps on each trade:

Step 1: Find the Extreme
    a. Calculate minimum volatility threshold
    b. Screen for Fast Movers
    c. Define your stock basket
    d. Pick your RSI
Step 2: Frame the Trade
    a. Set your contingency
    b. Size the position
    c. Put on the trade
Step 3: Book the Profit
    a. Sell signal
    – OR—
    b. Trailing stop

Now, let's see how this all plays out in real life by walking through some actual 10-Minute Millionaire trades step-by-step.

The examples I'm about to show you are based on trade recommendations that I actually made for my newsletter subscribers at Money Map Press LLC. I believe quite strongly in the 10-Minute Millionaire Rubber Band strategy and the underlying principles that I've outlined for you in this book. I believe in this strategy so much that it represents a foundational element of my newsletter action alerts.

To simplify the examples, instead of using language like "I signaled newsletter subscribers," I'll describe the trade in the first person. Also, some of the examples that follow show simplified Framing the Trade and Booking the Profit parameters so that they form better training models for you as you learn the system here in the book (especially where the newsletter parameters were a bit more sophisticated). So let's jump in to see how the 10-Minute Millionaire functions in real time.

Our first example trade is a great illustration of a textbook Rubber Band trade that worked out in nearly perfect fashion. The 10-Minute Millionaire system signaled an extreme pullback on an otherwise strong stock that immediately snapped back to trigger a definitive sell signal for a huge short-term profit. It doesn't get any more straightforward than that.

Once we walk through this case study, I'll show you several other trades that are a bit more complex in nature. These illustrate the value of system discipline and risk controls.

Let's start with the first trade.

Cleared for Take-off

During the first half of 2015, I ran my standard volatility screen—looking for some new stocks to add to my tracking basket. As usual, that screen took a mere 10 minutes to run.

Just to remind you: I was looking for stocks showing short-term volatility at least double the broader market that had enough trading volume to be relatively liquid.

At the time, the Standard & Poor's 500 Index was trading at 2,067 on a 14-day ATR of 19.24. A simple calculation showed me that my minimum volatility threshold was 0.019, or 1.9 percent of the price (see the following example).

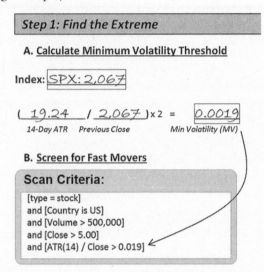

Step 1: Find the Extreme

A. Calculate Minimum Volatility Threshold

Index: SPX: 2,067

(19.24 / 2,067) x 2 = 0.0019

14-Day ATR   Previous Close   Min Volatility (MV)

B. Screen for Fast Movers

Scan Criteria:

[type = stock]
and [Country is US]
and [Volume > 500,000]
and [Close > 5.00]
and [ATR(14) / Close > 0.019]

Online travel company Expedia (Nasdaq: EXPE) popped up on my screen with volatility nearly 2.5 times my minimum. Intrigued, I took a closer look. (See Figure 8.1.) Sure enough, EXPE was manifesting some really interesting trading behavior. Every month or so, my charts showed me that traders seemed to jump on a selling bandwagon—pulling the stock into an extreme oversold situation. Almost on cue, the raucous rabble-rousers would get serious—and Expedia would suddenly snap back and run to new highs.

These are the precise situations that fire up the 10-Minute Millionaire. Clearly, extreme forces were at work here. So I put Expedia on my watch list in order to scope out the next opportunity.

I didn't have long to wait.

On July 27, EXPE dropped an aggregate $7-plus a share in just two days. The stock was still in a long-term uptrend, continuing its volatile behavior. My RSI indicator dipped below 5.0, and I knew it was time to pounce.

Remember: we never even *think* about doing a trade without being certain of our exit plan. So I started calculating my contingency exit by taking the three-day low and subtracting 1.0 times the current *Average True Range (ATR)*.

Figure 8.1 Snapback
SOURCE: Chart courtesy of StockCharts.com

In this case, the three-day low was $103.11. Subtracting the current ATR of 2.47 gave me a hard stop of $100.64—more than $5 a share below the current trading price.

Step 2: Frame the Trade							
A. Set Your Contingency Exit							
Symbol	Price	200-Day SMA	RSI	3-Day Low	14-Day ATR	Stop (Low − 1 x ATR)	Max Loss (Price − Stop)
EXPE	$105.80	$92.93	4.48	$103.11	$2.47	$100.64	$5.16

With my contingency exit fully planned, my next step was to *size* the position. Since I was willing to risk $500 on the trade, I ran the simple calculation and divided my *dollars at risk* by my *maximum loss per share* and came up with a *position size* of 100 shares.

A. Set Your Contingency Exit

Symbol	Price	200-Day SMA	RSI	3-Day Low	14-Day ATR	Stop (Low – 1 x ATR)	Max Loss (Price – Stop)
EXPE	$105.80	$92.93	4.48	$103.11	$2.47	$100.64	$5.16

B. Size the Position $500.00 / $5.16 = ⟦ 100 ⟧

                Dollars to Risk   *Max Loss*   *# of Shares*

Finally, I ran through my pretrade checklist.

Did you Find the Extreme by identifying a target stock that is:

• Showing recent volatility at least twice the broader market?
• Trading above its 200-day moving average?
• Displaying a three-day (or two-day) RSI lower than 10 (or even 5.0)?

Did you successfully frame your trade by:

• Identifying your contingency exit based on ATR?
• Calculating your maximum downside based on the stop-loss price?
• Determining your optimal position size in shares based on your risk tolerance?

Now, I was ready to pull the trigger. So I entered a market order at the open and immediately put in my stop-loss order as soon as the trade filled. Here's how my completed trading worksheet looked.

C. Put on the Trade

On _7/28/15_ at _9:30am_, I bought _100_ shares of _EXPE_ at _$105.80_ using a
     (Date)   *(Time)*   *(Quantity)*   *(Stock Symbol)*   *(Price)*

Market order for a total position size of _$10,580.00_. My stop is placed at _$100.64_ .
  (Order Type)   *(Dollars)*   *(Price)*

> **I PROMISE TO HONOR MY STOP.** _DRB_ *(Initials)*

Figure 8.2 illustrates graphically how the trade was framed.

Then, I walked away from my trade station—knowing my position was secure. If the trade played out as expected, I'd see a nice snapback in a few days or weeks. If the stock continued down, my potential losses were capped by my preplaced contingency stop.

Figure 8.2   Framing the Trade
SOURCE: Chart courtesy of StockCharts.com

It didn't take long to figure out what would happen. Within a couple of days, Expedia was up.

And it was up big. (See Figure 8.3.)

Figure 8.3   Booking the Profit
SOURCE: Chart courtesy of StockCharts.com

The stock gapped to the upside on July 31, closing at $120.40. The next trading day—August 3—Expedia's RSI hit 98.21, representing a super-overbought situation and a clear sell (for a profit) signal. Without questioning the situation (and trusting my system), I immediately sold my entire position at the market and canceled my stop order.

In the end, I booked a gross profit of better than $1,600 on a 100-share trade with only about $500 at risk. That represents a return that's better than three times my amount at risk. And it works out to a 15.17 percent gain in a mere six trading days—the kind of win that a buy-and-hold investor only dreams about.

Step 3: Book the Profit						
Date	Price	RSI	Trailing Stop	Gross Proceeds	Net Gain / (Loss)	% Gain / (Loss)
8/3/15	$121.85	98.21	N/A	$12,185.00	$1,605.00	15.2%

Let me put a fine point on what I'm talking about here.

And I'll do it by posing a riddle: When is a 15.17 percent return actually not a 15.17 percent return?

The answer: when it's a *637 percent return.*

Because that's what you have when you pull down a 15 percent profit in six days.

You see, there are 252 trading days in a year (about the average for the New York Stock Exchange and Nasdaq). Here's how that time span turns that Expedia profit into an annualized gain of about 637 percent (252 trading days / a six-day trade = a multiplier of 42. That multiplier of 42 × our 15.17 percent gain = an annualized return of 637 percent).

We annualize these gains to illustrate the true power that a trading system like this one has over a conventional buy-and-hold strategy.

Remember our illuminating story back in Chapter 3 about the true nature of slugger Babe Ruth—how he understood that by stringing together singles and doubles, he would become the potent force whose results were augmented by the towering homers that he also hit.

Those homers will come.

But if you truly want to achieve millionaire status—the stock market equivalent of Major League Baseball's Hall of Fame at Cooperstown— then you really want to amass the long strings of winning trades that are to a trader what singles, doubles, and triples are to a major leaguer.

With a trading system like mine, once you pull down a short-term gain (and close the trade), that represents a now greater amount of money that can be redeployed to a new opportunity. If we assume that the amount of capital you have available increases with each trade (on average, even after factoring out the money surrendered in risk-managed losing trades), you can see how your trading account can grow in value surprisingly quickly.

So while you'll crack some homers—some big wins on individual trades—of your own, what you'll really come to realize is this...

The singles and doubles that you consistently pick off—once annualized—*are* home runs. Especially when you string them together, one after the other.

In fact, here's another little story—quirky, but also interesting—that underscores this point.

A few years back, the business news site Quartz.com published a story called "How You Could Have Turned $1,000 into Billions of Dollars by Perfectly Trading the S&P 500 This Year."

In that piece, the writer posed this question: "What if you could put all of your eggs in one basket and never lose? How much could you have made in 2013 if you started with $1,000 to invest?"

The answer will stagger you—because we're talking about that thousand bucks turning into $264 billion... over the course of a single year.

Wrote Quartz.com's David Yanofsky, the author of that piece: "A trader who began the year with $1,000 in her brokerage account and put all of her money in each day's best-performing equity in the S&P 500—day after day—for the 241 trading days so far this year would have $264 billion in her account today."

As nice as it is to dream, we all recognize that no trader will put together 241 consecutive winning trades. Nor are you going to turn $1,000 into $264 billion.

You won't even turn that thousand bucks into $2.64 billion.

But here's the twist: a million dollars—even multiples of that million dollars—is a goal that is within reach.

There's also a lesson here—and it's an important one.

What this pie-in-the-sky (and fun) Quartz.com exercise does manage to do (albeit it in an extreme way) is illustrate the power of stringing together a series of short-duration, high-profit trades.

Indeed, as we explained as part of our sample Expedia trade, that's exactly what the 10-Minute Millionaire system was designed to do.

And if you string together enough of those short-duration, high-profit wins, you'll be well on your way to that first million dollars.

In fact, while not *every* 10-Minute Millionaire trade works out as spectacularly as Expedia—trades like this aren't uncommon at all . . .

Soon you'll be booking wins like that one on a regular basis. But you'll still be able to sleep at night, knowing that your risks are being controlled, that you have a market Edge, and that your capital is protected.

The risk-management aspects here (both on individual trades, and on your block of investment capital) are critical to understand. On the individual trades, the focus on managing risk cuts your losers short—so that they don't cancel out your winners. And the risk-management component of the strategy also makes sure you don't overreach—overcommit—with your capital . . . a miscue the pros refer to as "blowing yourself up."

With the 10-Minute Millionaire system, you're protected from such misadventures.

In the next example, I'll share a trade that illustrates the protective nature of this system.

Drug Enforcement

It's important to remember that even when the 10-Minute Millionaire has positive Edge—which includes a high probability of success—on every trade, that doesn't mean we'll win every time.

But that's okay.

With the proper contingency plans and risk controls in place, Rubber Band trades that break down instead of snapping back won't prove fatal to your financial well-being.

Indeed, you'll barely even feel the sting.

I have a great case study for you here—a trade I put on in the summer of 2015 that illustrates both the importance of contingency exits and the agony of a stop-out (a position that hits a well-placed stop-loss and then rebounds for a gain).

Luckily, this trade features a bit of redemption at the very end—a bonus, of sorts.

You'll see what I mean in a moment. But let's first set the stage.

As the New Year began in 2015, generic drug maker Mylan NV (Nasdaq: MYL) was kind of in a sleeper mode. For months, Mylan's shares had been trading around the mid-50s on light volume without much movement. It was almost like traders had been lulled to sleep by the monotonous predictability of a company with 1,400 different products (ranging from blood pressure pills to EpiPens to asthma inhalers) rolling off its production line.

In early April 2015, Mylan broke that monotony . . . in a big way.

Mylan offered to purchase generic drug giant Perrigo Co. PLC (NYSE: PRGO) for $205 per share. The buyout bid represented a 25 percent premium over Perrigo's pre-offer trading price of $162 a share.

The next day, Perrigo and Mylan both saw their share prices rocket 20 percent or more—and on heavy volume.

That pop would have represented a handsome profit for someone already holding the shares.

But, as is usually the case, this news-driven event came without warning. Only illegal inside information would have provided a decisive Edge. Like the trout fishermen bagging monster rainbows just downstream, it was a trade that fell outside of the 10-Minute Millionaire's target set at the time.

In short, we're talking about pure luck.

That's okay. If there's anything I've learned in my decades of trading, opportunities come around all the time. There's no sense switching tactics to chase the hot stock *du jour.* Sticking to a proven system is the way to catch what my dad referred to as our fair share, to keep risk in check—and to stay out of trouble.

What the surprise announcement *did* do, was to ignite a significant increase in short-term volatility, which landed Mylan on my Fast Mover list of stocks that warranted further evaluation.

Then, on April 21, 2015, the Israeli drug giant Teva Pharmaceutical Industries Ltd. (NYSE ADR: TEVA) unveiled a $40 billion (that's *billion* with a "B") unsolicited takeover bid for Mylan—a cash-and-stock offer worth $82 per share.

Mylan—the usually sleepy drug-sector giant that seemed to be heavily dosed on Ambien—was suddenly going hyperactive. And that's a great thing for the 10-Minute Millionaire. Big news and a kinetic M&A environment opens the sluice gate of information flow—an element of emotional market biases that show up as trading extremes.

By now, I was paying close attention for a good setup opportunity.

On June 17, 2015, Mylan pulled back a few points from an established trading range still well north of its 200-day SMA. (See Figure 8.4.) The two-day RSI had tanked to 5.54, and I was staring at a very nice high-quality setup.

This was clearly a market overreaction to some rumor—or the irrational herd mentality in its purest sense. The 10-Minute Millionaire system's signal was enough to flag the opportunity, but there was a subjective element to my analysis, too—specifically, Teva's standing $82-a-share offer for Mylan. Once traders returned to market reality, I figured they'd realize that Teva's bid represented a huge enough gravitational pull for them to shoot Mylan's shares back up.

With this insight—and the system data I had in hand—I was ready to Frame the Trade.

Figure 8.4   Finding the Extreme
SOURCE: Chart courtesy of StockCharts.com

First, I calculated the contingency stop at 1.5 times ATR below the three-day low of $71.18. Remember, you can choose a stop-loss level from 1.0 times ATR up to 2.0 times—with the following trade-offs:

Beginner	Intermediate	Advanced
1.0 × ATR	1.5 × ATR	2.0 × ATR
Tight	Medium	Loose
Lower average loss	Good compromise	Higher win rate

I chose the medium level at 1.5 times. The stock had good upside potential because of the merger action—at least to $82, and maybe higher if the situation sparked a bidding war. With all the moving parts—and all the uncertainty—I wanted also to give the stock some extra room to fluctuate while still limiting my downside to a modest level.

Next, I *sized the position* using my just-calculated stop price. I was willing to risk $250 on the trade, so that gave me a position size of about 85 shares.

All systems were go, so I pulled the trigger and put on the trade at the open, filling my 85-share market order at $71.72.

Here's how it looked on my trading worksheet:

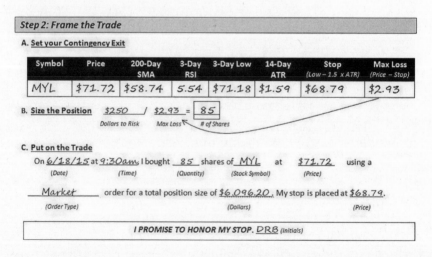

And Figure 8.5 shows what it looked like graphically on June 18.

Figure 8.5   Framing the Trade
SOURCE: Chart courtesy of StockCharts.com

The next day, Mylan ticked up about a point and showed increased relative strength of about 50. Since the RSI wasn't yet past my threshold of 80—and the price wasn't high enough to bump up a trailing stop, I was in a Condition Number 2 trade and simply stood pat.

The stock drifted down over the next few days, but stayed above my contingency exit. Then, on June 29, Mylan broke down and hit my stop at $68.79. (See Figure 8.6.) I was out of the trade with a modest—and acceptable (according to the system)—loss of 4.1 percent.

Here, however, I wanted us to look back together, because there's a lesson.

Even after my Mylan trade had closed out, the merger storyline kept me intrigued. So I watched to see how this saga played out.

Initially, at least, Mylan looked to be what Wall Street pros refer to as a "classic stop-out trade." I'd just been taken out at my stop price, and watched as Mylan reversed course and spiked more than 7 percent in five days.

Without a system—or if I was willing to fudge my stops . . . or had no contingency exit in the first place . . . and had I acted on the RSI sell trigger on July 6—I would have exited this trade at about breakeven.

Figure 8.6 Stop-Loss Hit
SOURCE: Chart courtesy of StockCharts.com

Or, like so many traders, I could have stuck with the trade, rationalizing that I'd eventually end up with a gain—perhaps even a big gain.

Instead, as I said earlier, I trusted my system, accepted risk-managed losses, and willingly moved on to the next trade.

Just like I tell new traders.

And here's where the vindication—of my system, and of my determination to trust that system—comes into our story.

On July 27, the Teva deal imploded. Mylan gapped down—plunging more than $20 a share from the interim high the stock had hit just two weeks earlier. (See Figure 8.7.)

Had I jettisoned my approach to the markets and stuck with the trade, my loss would have been almost eight times bigger than the small, risk-managed loss I accepted by trusting my trading system. A mistake of that magnitude can take a trader *months*—or longer—to recover from.

I trusted my system, and accepted a small loss—and thereby dodged a huge loss. It was easy for me to move on to my next trade.

Figure 8.7   Loss Avoided
Source: Chart courtesy of StockCharts.com

Call it a "happy ending in disguise."

And here, in our final case study, is a trade that had a true, clear, and profitable happy ending.

Game On

During the early months of 2015, video game maker Electronic Arts Inc. (Nasdaq: EA) had been relatively sedate and off my radar with a volatility ratio (0.018) well below my trading threshold.

In late July 2015, the stock started experiencing more volatility. EA's *ATR/Price ratio* rose from 0.016 to 0.023 in early August on strong trading volume between three million to five million shares a day—which easily met my liquidity requirements. At its level in the low $70s, Electronic Arts' stock price made my minimum-price rule a moot point. So the stock was listed in my screening basket as a potential Fast Mover for future monitoring.

Step 1: Find the Extreme

A. Calculate Minimum Volatility Threshold

Index: SPX: 2,111

(18.90 / 2,111) x 2 = 0.018

14-Day ATR   Previous Close   Min Volatility (MV)

B. Screen for Fast Movers

Scan Criteria:

[type = stock]
and [Country is US]
and [SMA(14, Volume) > 500,000]
and [Close > 5.00]
and [ATR(14) / Close > 0.018]

C. Define Your Stock Basket

Fast Movers with Extreme Potential (Symbols)				
FLSR	EXPE	EA	GOOG	SHAK

D. Pick Your RSI

Option #1	Option #2
RSI < 10	RSI < 5
• More Trades	• Fewer Trades
• Lower % Return	• Higher % Return

By late August of that year, crude oil had dropped below the $40-a-barrel level. And China devalued its currency. The one-two punch pushed the stock market off the ledge and into a total freefall.

Coming off of a 200 percent gain since the Great Recession of 2007–2009, stocks were susceptible to a hefty correction. On August 21, 2015, a Friday, the S&P 500 closed on its low of the day, down 64 points from the open and down 130 from its close earlier that week.

EA closed at $65.53, about a point and a half off of its lows for that day. The stock was still trading above its 200-day moving average. But the three-day RSI indicator had taken a recent nosedive below 5.0— meaning it was in extreme oversold territory. While others might have been spooked to buy into a sharp selloff, to me it looked like a classic Rubber Band setup.

I had the weekend to study the chart and plan my next move.

On Monday August 24, 2015, EA opened at $60.25 (see Figure 8.8). It still looked like an ideal Rubber Band setup so I quickly did the math.

First, I set my contingency exit and calculated a stop price at $58.00, exactly 1.0 × ATR below the current stock price (which also happened to be the low of the last three trading days).

For the sake of illustration, let's say I was willing to risk $250 on the trade. With a potential loss of $2.25 per share if I got stopped out, I sized the position at 110 shares ($250/$2.25 = 111 shares) rounded down for simplicity.

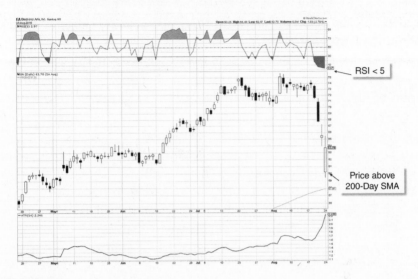

Figure 8.8 Finding the Extreme
SOURCE: Chart courtesy of StockCharts.com

Finally, after running through my pre-flight checklist, I put on the trade with a market order, which filled at $60.25. I immediately put my stop in place.

Step 2: Frame the Trade

A. Set Your Contingency

Symbol	Price	200-Day SMA	RSI	3-Day Low	14-Day ATR	Stop (Low − 1 x ATR)	Max Loss (Price − Stop)
EA	$60.25	$57.91	2.97	$60.25	$2.25	$58.00	$2.25

B. Size the Position $250.00 / $2.25 = 111

Dollars to Risk   Max Loss   # of Shares

C. Enter the Trade

On 8/24/15 at 9:01am, I bought 110 shares of EA at $60.25 using a

(Date)   (Time)   (Quantity)   (Stock Symbol)   (Price)

Market order for a total position size of $6,627.50. My stop is placed at $58.00.

(Order Type)   (Dollars)   (Price)

I PROMISE TO HONOR MY STOP. DRB (Initials)

That day, Electronic Arts bottomed out at $59.47 (more than a full point above my contingency) and closed up more than three bucks a share at $63.70. Had I been like most amateur traders—and taken my profits too soon—I would have grossed a cool $379.50 for nearly a

6 percent gain in a single day. Not too shabby, but also not the way of the 10-Minute Millionaire.

Over the next two weeks, both EA's stock price and RSI strengthened. On August 28, 2015, the stock closed at $66.51 on an RSI just short of my profit-booking threshold of 80.

So I stood pat.

The following week, the stock sold off again slightly.

In my formative trading years, I might have panicked at that point, second-guessed my decision not to fudge my RSI sell trigger after that August 28 bump, and locked in my gains rather than risk a loss.

Years (and lots of research and experience) later, I still trust my system. I know it works. And soon enough, you will, too.

So instead of selling outright, I set a trailing stop at $62.53, which was 1.5 times ATR below the $65.98 intermediate low on August 31. At this point, my trade was all but guaranteed to be profitable. Even if EA continued to sell off, I'd still book a 4 percent profit.

That may not sound like a lot.

But look at it this way.

If I could book a 4 percent gain every two weeks with such nominal risks, *I'd more than double my money in a year.*

That's the power of compounding at work.

And here's the math that illustrates it.

As our starting point, let's use the $6,627.50 position that I took in the Electronic Arts trade example we just talked about.

The first 4 percent win gets you to $6,892.50 ($6,627.50 × 1.04 = $6,892.60). The second gets you to $7,168.30 ($6,892.60 × 1.04 = $7,168.30). Do that multiplication series 26 times (I said you only needed to do this every two weeks) and you have more than twice as much as you started with.

Here, in fact, you'd end up with $18,374.54.

Like our earlier Quartz.com example, this is an extreme example. But it also shows what you can achieve by stringing together a bunch of wins (even when those wins are modest).

It's not the individual wins themselves, but the fact that you keep doing it—which is why my system is designed to help you, too.

Just think how you would have done had you started with an even bigger stake—and doubled that. Or if you took an underperforming slice of your overall portfolio and doubled that.

Impressive stuff.

But on my Electronic Arts trade, my system told me to expect *more* than that 4 percent.

EA did sell off the next day—and even gapped down—but I was protected. My ATR-based trailing stop was in place but never got hit. Either way, I was okay. My profit on the trade would be either *good* or *great*. My system had predicted a big snapback, so I was sticking with the trade.

Sure enough, on September 8, 2015, EA closed at $68.50 on a three-day RSI of 81.51. (See Figure 8.9.) It was time to Book the Profit. I entered a sell order at open on September 9, which filled at $69.54 for a 15.4 percent pop and a gain of more than $1,000.

That 16-day trade represented an annualized gain of nearly 300 percent. Here's the math.

(252 trading days / 16-day trade = 15.75 multiplier × 15.4 percent profit = annualized profit of 243 percent)

With $250 at risk, it was an amazing Edge and a downright excellent trade.

Figure 8.9 Trailing Stop
SOURCE: Chart courtesy of StockCharts.com

| Step 3: Book the Profit | | | | | | |
Date	Price	RSI	Trailing Stop	Gross Proceeds	Net Gain / (Loss)	% Gain / (Loss)
9/9/15	$69.54	81.51	62.53	$7,649.40	$1,021.90	15.4%

The key takeaway: this is a system that will let you string together a series of profitable trades (even after you've subtracted the risk-adjusted losers)—putting you on the freeway to millionaire status.

And that's the key point: this is a trading system—a carefully designed approach to the stock market—that's designed to allow you to capture big annualized gains. I'm talking about a series of short-term wins that, strung together, will get you to the promised land (millionaire status)—and in a truncated time frame that could *never* be achieved by conventional buy-and-hold strategies.

Now it's time for you to take that first step.

It's "Self-Improvement"...
Not "Shelf Improvement"

The secret to getting ahead is getting started.

—Mark Twain

I'd be willing to wager that everyone reading this—at one time or another in his or her life—has dreamed of being wealthy.

And that's totally understandable...it's a great dream.

Unfortunately, most of those same folks never turned that dream into an actual goal—figuring it was unrealistic...and unattainable.

But it's not.

In fact, as dreams go . . . it's very attainable.

As Mark Twain said so long ago . . . the first step is getting started.

I've made a very similar point to the many folks I've talked with during my seminars down through the years. And I'll reiterate the point to each of you here now.

You bought this book. And you took the time to read it and contemplate its message.

But now you must decide whether that effort was for self-improvement (I'm putting this strategy into effect right now) or "shelf improvement" (D. R.'s book will make a nice addition to my personal investment library).

I'll argue that the self-improvement should win out over the shelf-improvement every time—and for one very good reason.

The wealth you can accumulate from this strategy will make it possible to attain so many of the *other* dreams and goals that I know each of you has.

So allow me to leave you with three final thoughts—which I like to refer to as my 10-Minute Millionaire Takeaways.

They consist of:

1. **10-Minute Millionaire Takeaway Number 1: Don't Be a Donkey.** This old story is a favorite of mine, and actually dates all the way back to Aristotle. Known in philosophy as the Paradox of Buridan's Ass, it's actually something most of you might recognize as "paralysis by analysis." If you're not familiar with this parable, it was named for fourteenth-century French priest and philosopher Jean Buridan who studied under famed simplifier William of Ockham. The paradox goes something like this: a donkey (the modern-day name of the animal) finds itself equidistant from two, identical and delicious piles of hay. Not being able to tell which pile of hay is better, the donkey starves to death within easy reach of the food that could have easily sustained it. Investors do the same thing. Intelligent men and women who know they need to start investing—for retirement, for college for their kids, for taking care of their aging parents—study the dickens out of stocks, the economy, and the broad markets, looking for the best time to start. Ultimately, they opt to postpone the start of their investing program until the market environment

becomes clear. In doing so, they literally starve themselves of potential (and needed) wealth. And when they look back 20 years later, they realize the truth that any time would have been a fine starting point. *The Key Point: Just get started. Now. Don't overthink it. The 10-Minute Millionaire system is designed to boost your upside while minimizing your risk. And you'll have the opportunity for money aplenty—which is always better than starving.*

2. 10-Minute Millionaire Takeaway Number 2: Once You Start, Stay the Course. Although he didn't invent the saying "don't change horses in midstream," U.S. President Abraham Lincoln popularized it during his 1864 reelection campaign. Indeed, back then, it was actually written as "don't swap horses in the middle of the stream." The modernization aside, the meaning is clear. President Lincoln was seeking a second term while the U.S. Civil War was still being waged. In this slogan, Lincoln's presidency and policies—and the future of the country—were all represented by the rider halfway across the running stream. And he was warning of the huge potential risks of changing direction with the job (winning the war) not yet finished. The slogan—and the focus on Lincoln's very real first-term achievements—helped him win a second term, with 55 percent of the popular vote. And he was able to traverse the rest of the stream and finish the job he'd started. This bit of history really resonates with me—and for good reason. If not starting at all is the biggest miscue I see investors make, then playing a game of "investment strategy musical chairs" is a close second. Investors will start out as value players, then get seduced by momentum, then migrate to small caps, then shift to indexing—always chasing the current hot strategy. The trouble is, these investors usually end up changing horses at the worst possible moment—when the formerly hot strategy goes cold. And by doing this over and over again, the results they achieve are disastrous. *The Key Point: If you decide to adopt the 10-Minute Millionaire strategy, stick with it. Carve out the 10-minute stretches it takes to keep your wealth-building program going. There will be tough stretches. That's normal. But if you stick with this, give the strategy time to work in your favor, and work it like it's designed, you'll find that your probabilities for generating market-trouncing results over the long haul rise accordingly. And you'll find that this system, once up and running, requires very small*

time investments to maintain. Most important of all, remember that when you change horses in midstream, sometimes you fall off. . . and get washed downstream—maybe even farther back than when you started. And that's a wasteful outcome we all wish to avoid.

3. **10-Minute Millionaire Takeaway Number 3: Always Remember That Money Is a Means to an End. . . Not the End Itself.** Early in this book—when recounting the lessons I've learned from the world's billionaires—I mentioned that one of the most important lessons of all was to be grateful for what you have. That lesson goes double once you've reached millionaire status. Take the time to enjoy what the money brings you. . . the security it brings your family. . . the ability it gives you to help your community. . . and the time it gives you to truly enjoy your life. For me, this has been one of the most gratifying parts of all. I've seen the rewards other followers of my system have reaped. And I've reaped those rewards myself—which is why I've made sure to give back. In addition to the stocks and investment coaching I've done with elementary school kids, I've also coached basketball and 13 years ago even started the Newark Charter Middle School JV team. And for a week every summer, I teach at Camp Pecometh—which gets kids out of the inner city and suburbs and into a wonderful riverside campground as part of a yearly program run by a longtime friend. Truth be told. . . when I watch the kids, what they're learning and the fun they're having, I often feel like I'm getting the better part of the bargain. *The Key Point: Seeing money as a means not an end—having a bigger "why"—will allow you to persevere through the occasional tough time. And once the 10-Minute Millionaire strategy gets you to where you want to be, take the time to appreciate what you've achieved. And pay it forward, by helping those who may not be as fortunate. You'll feel great and will be surprised when your truly selfless acts seem to pay dividends. And don't minimize the impact of what you're doing. As Mother Teresa once said, "We know only too well that what we are doing is nothing more than a drop in the ocean. But if the drop were not there, the ocean would be missing something."*

As you start your journey, I wish you—and those who are important to you—the very best.

APPENDIX

The 10-Minute Millionaire's Trading Worksheet

Date: _____

A. Calculate Minimum Volatility Threshold

Index: [   ]

(_____ / _____) x 2 = [   ]
14-Day ATR Previous Close   Min Volatility (MV)

B. Screen for Fast Movers

Scan Criteria:

[type = stock]
and [SMA(14, Volume) > 500,000]
and [Close > 5.00]
and [ATR(14) / Close > MV]

C. Define Your Stock Basket

Fast Movers with Extreme Potential (Symbols)			

D. Pick Your RSI

Option #1	Option #2
RSI < 10	RSI < 5
• More Trades	• Fewer Trades
• Lower % Return	• Higher % Return

Step 2: Frame the Trade

A. Set Your Contingency

Symbol	Price	200-Day SMA	RSI	3-Day Low	14-Day ATR	Stop (Low – 1 x ATR)	Max Loss (Price – Stop)

B. Size the Position $ _____ / $ _____ = [   ]
Dollars to Risk   Max Loss   # of Shares

C. Put on the Trade

On _____ at _____, I bought _____ shares of _____ at $ _____ using a
(Date)   (Time)   (Quantity)   (Stock Symbol)   (Price)

_____ order for a total position size of $ _____. My stop is placed at $ _____.
(Order Type)   (Dollars)   (Price)

I PROMISE TO HONOR MY STOP. _____ (Initials)

Step 3: Book the Profit

Date	Price	RSI	Trailing Stop	Gross Proceeds	Net Gain / (Loss)	% Gain / (Loss)

Notes:

GLOSSARY

Term	Definition
10-Minute Millionaire	a) A systematic approach to trading designed to repeatedly and reliably generate short-term profits to build long-term wealth by capitalizing on market extremes in as little as 10 minutes per day. b) A practitioner of the 10-Minute Millionaire system.
Ask	The price at which traders are willing to sell a security.
Auction	A marketplace in which the price is neither set nor arrived at by negotiation, but is instead discovered through competitive and open bidding by emotion-driven, psychologically irrational human beings.
Average True Range (ATR)	A measure of short-term volatility that represents the actual trading range of a security over a specified period, including intraday gaps.
Beta	a) A measure of long-term volatility in relation to a broad market index used frequently in portfolio management. b) An unsuitable volatility metric for short-term trading of extremes.
Bid	The price at which traders are willing to buy a security.
Contingency Exit	A planned exit point for a trade; often synonymous with stop-loss.

Term	Definition
Conventional Wisdom	A common set of beliefs—shared by the majority of the populace—that are usually dead wrong. But they are nevertheless dangerous because they possess the air of truth.
Downside Risk	The presumed maximum potential loss on a trade as governed by the contingency exit.
Edge	A measure of positive expectancy. Mathematically: Edge = Expected Return − Downside Risk.
Efficient Markets Hypothesis (EMH)	A widely held (and largely false) belief that market prices are perfectly efficient in that they represent the fair value of an underlying security at any given moment. This also posits a complete and instantaneous dissemination of information between buyers and sellers. According to EMH, any investment outperformance is purely a function of chance.
Expected Return	The sum of all potential gains or losses predicted by a trading approach, each multiplied by the probability of its occurrence. Individual trade returns will vary, but over many trades, the average of a trader's overall results will converge on the expected return.
Extreme	a) A condition of market overreaction in which prices are stretched or pulled quickly and irrationally away from a reasonable market value. b) Out of whack; crazy. c) A trading opportunity with high profit potential.
Gambler's Fallacy	The irrational belief that a streak of random occurrences will reverse—or is somehow due for a correction.
Gap	A trading condition in which the trading range of a stock or other security falls entirely outside the previous day's range. The resultant trading chart is marked by a blank area between trading days with no price points recorded in the gap range. Opening gaps are a subset in which the price between the close of stock or other investment security and its open is significant.
Herd	a) A group of dumb cattle. b) A group of traders seeming to act in unison because of emotionally driven collective peer influence.
Irrational	a) The absence of logic and rational thought. b) A mental state in humans thought to occur when the primitive limbic system of the brain hijacks the higher analytical functions of the prefrontal cortex, leading to poor decision making.

Term	Definition
	c) A state of being that successful investors seek to avoid in themselves and profit from in others.
Limit Order	A standing order to buy or sell a stock or other security at a specified price or better.
Liquidity	A measure of the degree to which a stock or security can be traded in the market at stable price levels. See also: Spread, Volume.
Long-Term	Months, years, decades.
Loss Aversion Bias	The scientifically proven human bias to value the avoidance of a loss much more than the receipt of a gain.
Market	An aggregation of humans—many of them irrational—who are attempting to use the auction format to buy or sell securities, commodities, or other assets in pursuit of profit. See also: Auction.
Market Order	An order to buy or sell a specified number of shares of a security or other trading instrument at the prevailing market price at the moment of execution.
Minimum Volatility	The lowest-allowable level of short-term fluctuation for a stock to be included in the 10-Minute Millionaire's basket of potential trading opportunities.
Minuteman	a) Reference to the members of America's early militiamen who were ready to fight on a minute's notice to capitalize on extreme opportunities for decisive victory against an enemy force shackled by conventional tactics and herd mentality. b) An inspirational metaphor for the 10-Minute Millionaire.
Overbought	A stock or other security that has been bid up to an extreme price level.
Oversold	A stock or other security that has been sold down to an extreme price level.
Position Size	a) The number of shares or contracts put on in any given trade as determined by, first, the trader's precalculated contingency exit and, second, tolerance for risk. b) The single most important factor of the 10-Minute Millionaire's risk control practices. c) The part of our system that answers the question: "How many shares or contracts?"
Positive Expectancy	Positive expected return over a large number of trades.

Term	Definition
Random Walk	a) A term born of the Efficient Markets Hypothesis coined by Burton G. Malkiel suggesting that market prices are completely random, devoid of irrational human influence, and cannot be predicted or profited from. b) The mantra of index fund employees and buy-and-hold investors worldwide. c) See: Conventional Wisdom.
Relative Strength Indicator (RSI)	A momentum oscillator developed by J. Welles Wilder that measures the speed of change of price movements in a stock or other investment security. Signals oscillate between 0 and 100, with 70 or greater being widely considered overbought and 30 or less, oversold.
Results-Orientation Bias	A goal-setting behavior that can cause traders to break their system rules in order to achieve a stated objective (that is, result). The 10-Minute Millionaire mindset is to have process-oriented goals (follow the system properly) that will lead to positive results over time.
Risk Tolerance	An individual trader's mental and financial ability to withstand a given loss on a trade.
Rubber Band	a) An oversold stock or other trading instrument poised for a sharp snapback for huge profit potential. b) The cornerstone extreme trading opportunity for the 10-Minute Millionaire.
Short-Term	Days, weeks.
Simple Moving Average (SMA)	A trend-identification technique used to smooth erratic price movements calculated by adding the closing price of a given security for a number of time periods and then dividing the total by the same number of time periods.
Spread	The difference between the bid and ask price of a marketable security; wide spreads indicate low liquidity, and vice versa.
Stop-Loss	The calculated price at which a stop order is entered for any given trade as determined by the trading-system parameters—and *not* by risk tolerance. See also: Contingency Exit.
Stop Order	An order to buy or sell a stock or other security once the price of the instrument reaches a specified price, known as the "stop price." When the stop price is reached, a stop order becomes a market order and will execute in full at the prevailing market price at the time.

Term	Definition
Stop Out	a) An occurrence expected to happen on a minority of trades when a stock price triggers the 10-Minute Millionaire's stop order. b) A counterintuitive opportunity to fortify one's resolve to honor your stop and reject conventional wisdom and irrational behavior.
Streak	A series of repeating outcomes in a random or probabilistic process. These occur more frequently and for a longer duration than we are programmed to expect.
Streak Bias	A human mental limitation leading to a belief that a short-term string of random occurrences indicates, first, a longer-term trend in the same direction, or, second, a complete trend reversal and a reversion to the mean. See also: Conventional Wisdom, Gambler's Fallacy.
System	a) A construct of human intelligence and ingenuity that can eliminate bias and human error from a process to generate consistent, repeatable, and reliable results. b) A money-making machine that, when run with discipline, provides the opportunity to generate enormous wealth in as little a time as 10 minutes per day.
Volatility	The degree to which a stock or security price varies over a specified period of time, often used as a measure of risk or of potential reward.
Volume	a) The number of shares or contracts exchanged on any given time period. b) A measure of liquidity.

INDEX